On Guard for Thee

Mark Macy

On Guard for Thee

ISBN: 1-59568-002-0

Published in the United States by
Beaufort Publishing Group
www.beaufortpublishinggroup.com

Dedication

I would like to dedicate this book to my father, mother, brothers and sister. Thank you for everything.

Love,
Mark

Acknowledgements

I sincerely wish to thank my family, close friends, and dedicated, loyal employees (past and present) for their inspiration and wisdom. They have reinforced and continue to reinforce my drive to succeed. Although life's circumstances have separated us, I'd also like to thank those people whose past lessons remain close to me today.

I further extend heartfelt thanks to the contributors who have generously given of their time and offered their insights to this project: Steve Hebert, Patrick Ogilvie, Glenn Thornley, Frank Kelly, Kathleen Nolan, Kevin Cooney, Dana Fleming and Erin Lang.

Finally, I would like to thank those individuals who have dedicated themselves to the realization of this book: to Mike Fabbro, for his excellent editorial assistance, to Sarah McGregor, who aided in the book's genesis and to Maya Bahar and Cecilia Blanchfield, whose writing skills and patience saw it through to its completion.

All my best wishes,

Mark Macy
President, North American Security Services

Table of Contents

Chapter One

The Mountain Man

Although the events I am about to describe may sound unbelievable, what follows is not the plot of an action movie. It is an entirely true story--unembellished. These are the straight goods, as they say.

It was the end of June. My close friend Eric and I intended to hike up Mount Royal, a large mountain in Fresno, Colorado. Eric was fairly experienced, but this was one of my first hikes.

That morning we figured it would take us about an hour and a half to get up the mountain and, of course, we expected the trip down to be shorter. So we threw a couple bottles of water, some nuts and a few pieces of fruit into our knapsacks. Now, Eric and I are known for our preparedness, especially at work, where we are extremely thorough and attentive. But this time we didn't give much thought to Murphy's Law--if it can go wrong, it will. In fact, we didn't even consider what might go wrong on our journey. When we set out on that beautiful sunny morning at 8 a.m., little did we know that we would not be returning a few hours later, as planned.

The time passed quickly, and we reached the end of the defined trail on schedule. Although the terrain had been steeper than what I was used to, I felt great. We drank some water and ate some fruit. I thanked Eric for the great excursion and started to get ready to go down again. But Eric was still raring to go; he suggested we continue all the way up to the summit; he wanted us to experience the feeling of reaching the peak. I was a bit skeptical at first, but then I thought: *Why not?* I was on vacation; I wanted to enjoy my holiday to the fullest. Besides, I've always been ready to take on new challenges.

So we resumed our upward climb, past the last bearings of the marked trail. Before we knew it, the trees were at armpit level and then at the level of our knees. Soon, we could see the summit in the distance. At 1 p.m., we had reached the top. It was really cold!

At the base of the mountain it had been 80 degrees, and we were hot. We'd been fine in our short-sleeved shirts, shorts and hiking boots. Now we were surrounded by ice and we could have used much warmer clothes. Nevertheless, we were exhilarated. We had reached the highest point on Mount Royal! We took in the amazing vistas as well as deep lungfuls of fresh air. I drank the rest of my water and ate what was left of my snacks. Eric left a few ounces of water in his bottle and asked me why I hadn't saved any of mine. "We have plenty more in the car," I said "and we'll be down soon." Or so I thought.

We decided it was time to descend. We headed for the same unmarked trail we had taken to get to this point. Unfortunately, after a few minutes, we realized that we were on a different slope, a scree slope. We were trying to make our way down a path made up of loose rocks and stones. Somehow we had gotten ourselves on the wrong side of the mountain.

We decided to continue for two reasons. First, going down the steep grade had been hard enough; we couldn't imagine having to climb back up. Second, although we were on the wrong side of the mountain, at least we were headed in the right direction: downwards! From where we stood, we could see the road many thousands of feet below us. We figured, once we got down, we could always hitchhike to where we had left the car.

As we went down, I took care to place my feet at an angle. Given the grade of the slope, we were forced to use the edge of our boots to keep from tripping or sliding. I'm an active person, but after just a few minutes of trying to keep my balance on the loose rocks, I was panting and gasping. We had to stop often to catch our breath. Eric suggested that we descend in parallel; he did not want me standing behind him or in front of him, a position where one of us could dislodge a rock that would hit the other.

Around 2:30 that afternoon, I had a sudden urge to stop in my tracks. I turned to Eric and told him to stop too. Something didn't look right. About 10 feet ahead, there was subtle change in the look of the slope. I edged my way forward very carefully, inches at a time. Eric froze, angling his boots to keep from sliding further. It was a good thing he did, because straight ahead of us was a drastic drop—a cliff! I told Eric to keep still. "What is it? What do you see?" he asked. "Stay where you are!" I said sharply. I moved very gingerly to the left to see if there was another way down the slope. On the left, I saw another cliff. So I cautiously edged my way to the right. Another cliff!

Eric was emphatic that our only option was to climb back up. I knew he was right, but it had taken us an hour to descend the slope as far as we had and we had been hiking for almost seven hours. I was exhausted.

Eric was ready to tackle what seemed to me like an insurmountable challenge. I just couldn't move. He looked at me, expecting me to follow, but I couldn't. My mouth and throat were parched. The afternoon sun was hitting the side of the mountain and it was painfully hot. I was so physically drained that I started mentally making preparations to die. It took what was left of my energy to croak out four words. "Go on without me," I said to Eric.

Eric however, refused to abandon me. Over and over, he shouted at me: "Come on! Climb! Move! Get up here!" "I can't," I managed to say. "I've got nothing left. I'm empty." "Climb! Climb!" he persisted. This went on for quite a while. And then something happened: I got my second wind. I got on my hands and knees and with the little strength that had come back to me, I began to crawl up the scree slope, grabbing rocks as they slid by. It took me quite a few minutes to reach my friend. Once I did, we started crawling up the mountain side by side, with him encouraging me all the way.

Every so often we would pause, and he would blow on the warning whistle that hung around his neck. I wasn't too optimistic that there would be anyone on this side of the mountain to hear it, and I told him so, but he kept blowing that annoying whistle.

Night fell around 9 p.m. and we were still on the wrong side of the mountain. Eric shared his last ounces of water with me. I needed fluids desperately; my muscles were cramping. I was so thirsty, I scooped up some snow to eat. The temperature dropped. Now we were freezing again, and we clung to each other for warmth. We both wondered: would we make it through the night? If cold and thirst and exhaustion didn't do us in, something else would. This was Colorado, after all, home of grizzly bears, wildcats and rattlesnakes.

That was the longest and the most unbearably cold night I have ever endured. The moment I saw a ray of light reflected off a nearby mountain, I jumped up "Where are you going?" Eric said, feeling colder without me. "We need to make a fire," I told him. I wasn't sure how I was going to do it, since my frozen fingers felt as it they were going to snap off. Somehow, I found some twigs, started a small fire and we got to warm our hands. I told Eric we had to push on to the top and find out where we had made that wrong turn the day before. But now it was Eric's turn to despair. "Don't give up. You can do this," I assured him. The day before, he had been the strong one; now it was my turn to buck him up.

"Eric", I said, "take five steps, just five steps. After we do that, we'll stop and we will wait until we're ready to take another five steps." So that's the way we did it. Five steps, followed by a two-minute pause to recoup. Another five small steps. Before we knew it, we were pushing ourselves a little more, taking seven steps, then 10, and then 15. The pauses grew shorter and shorter and finally we didn't stop at all.

With his breath back, Eric started blowing on the whistle again. I found the sound really aggravating. "Eric, there's no one on the mountain but you and me," I said, but he kept blowing that blasted whistle.

When we finally got up to the peak, we were ecstatic. It was about 11 a.m. and we'd been on the mountain for over 24 hours. Now, if only we could find the point where we had come up from the marked trail. Where was the safe path that we had taken the day before? While we looked around, Eric kept blowing his whistle.

Suddenly a man emerged from the dense brush. He was shirtless and carrying a large stick. He looked like he was comfortable in this environment and his confident stride told me that he was an experienced hiker. I turned to Eric and shouted: "We're saved!" "What are you talking about?" he said irritably.

Perhaps he thought I was losing my mind. Eric was about 100 feet away and couldn't see our savior from where he sat on a rock.

The true mountain guy, as I came to think of him, had heard the whistle. When we had blurted out our story, he told us we were lucky to be alive. He gave us his water; it hurt to drink it because my throat had almost closed up. He also gave us an apple which Eric and I shared. And he offered to help get us down. We told him we would pay him but he replied that it was unnecessary: Helping us was reward enough.

He quickly showed us the way to the marked trail that we had missed the day before. I felt indescribably relieved when I knew I was finally on the right path down. He stayed with us down to the foot of the mountain and once again, he rejected any offer of payment.

Our unplanned adventure had left us in pretty bad shape. Our feet were blistered and bleeding. There were splinters embedded in the skin of our hands and knees, and we were raw from sunburn. We spent more than three days recovering.

That experience could have turned me off hiking, but just the opposite is true. Today, I continue to hike. I love it. But now, whenever I hike, I am always prepared for the unexpected. I pack more supplies than I think I'm going to need and I carry a first aid kit. I make sure I notify others of my return time, and I always have some means of communication with me at all times.

As miserable as it was at the time, that hike turned out to be one of the most valuable experiences of my life. I learned some pretty important lessons that I continue to incorporate into my outdoor excursions, my work and other aspects of my life.

Since that day, life has presented me with many challenges, some of which seemed insurmountable at first. Some of these mountainous challenges were at work, and some in relationships. Whenever I feel as if I can't overcome an obstacle, I stop to think about how we got off that mountain.

We took five steps, we stopped and we breathed. Eric helped me and I in turn helped him. And of course, we were blessed to run into that "true mountain guy."

Today, I know that my team and I can meet any challenge. In our security business, for instance, the incredible growth that companies like Nortel Networks experienced put huge demands on us. We had to stretch our resources to meet the needs of their global initiatives. We had to work through other crises such as 9/11, massive ice storms and region-wide power outages. We succeeded by applying the skills that Eric and I had honed from our Mount Royal climb.

I would like to share these powerful strategies with you now. They have worked for me, and for others, countless times. I guarantee that if you think carefully about these strategies and apply them every day, you will not only enjoy your work as a security officer, but you will be better at it.

Chapter Two

The Five Key Elements of Success

Everything you value in life is protected by a measure of security.

As security officers, there are certain things you can do to be successful. I offer the following five pearls of wisdom that have served me well over the years. As shown in the first chapter, I sometimes forget my own advice, which is why I encourage you to review these elements periodically.

Preparedness

"I will prepare and some day my chance will come."
Abraham Lincoln

Safety and security are largely a matter of being prepared. When you are prepared, you can take action quickly and without hesitation. Also, you are less likely to panic.

But how do you become prepared?

When Eric and I went up Mount Royal, we obviously did not anticipate that a three-hour hike would turn into a 31-hour ordeal. Even so, we could have prevented much of the suffering we went through, had we **visualized** and **anticipated** the possibilities. Had we **imagined** that we might take a wrong turn, then we certainly would have been a lot more attentive to our surroundings during our journey up the mountain. We definitely would have packed additional supplies, and certainly more food and water. Had we **envisioned** that the temperature would be so dramatically different at higher altitudes, we certainly would have brought along warmer clothes. Foolishly, we assumed that things would simply go as planned.

As security officers, we must prepare for the unexpected. Never assume that things will go perfectly as planned. After all, we live in an imperfect world. One of the ways you can prepare yourself for a crisis is by **visualizing** a multiplicity of scenarios. Ask yourself, "How can I prepare myself for situation a, b or c?

How can I be prepared for every possibility?" By asking these crucial questions, you can prevent many problems, and minimize the adverse consequences of a crisis.

In addition to **visualizing** what could happen during your shifts, you can become better prepared to deal with a crisis by **drilling** and **rehearsing your responses.** Do this over and over again, so that if and when a crisis arises, your responses will be instinctive.

Think about some actions that are so habitual they feel instinctive. When I leave my house, for instance, I lock the door. I do not consciously have to think about the micro-steps involved, such as taking out my key chain, selecting the right key, putting it in the lock, turning the lock, taking the key out, and double-checking that the door is secure. I have done this so many times that I do it without thinking. In a sense, I'm on autopilot. As I write this, I have had to consciously think about the simple, micro-actions of locking the door. By doing so, I have become aware of each step involved in this instinctive action.

Okay, now let's turn this situation around. Let's imagine that you are being taught how to operate a sophisticated, multi-stage emergency building evacuation system, i.e. a fire-evacuation panel. You become prepared by first, thinking about what you want to achieve. **Expertise in execution comes from rehearsing and drilling each micro-step, and from practicing these steps in sequence.** Imagine that the fire alarm is going off in the building. You have visualized the many steps that you must perform, over and over again in your head. Indeed, during every shift, you have mentally rehearsed a mini-drill. Consequently, you don't feel panicked when the horns or bells start sounding.

Here's another example of preparedness: don't wait until someone around you suffers an injury or has a heart attack before you think of taking a CPR/first-aid course. This might seem obvious, but the possibility of tragedy certainly amplifies the need to be prepared. The crucial skills you learn will be yours for the rest of your life.

Or will they? Just because you are taught the basics and go through a structured program once, does not mean that you will necessarily retain these skills. The onus is on you to **practice** what you have learned, so that you will be proficient in an emergency.

I remember the first time I had to splint a broken wrist. Although I had completed my first-aid certification, I was still very anxious about having to stabilize the injured limb. Since that first incident, I have given first aid to well over 100 people on and off the job. **I cannot over-emphasize the need to constantly rehearse and review the fundamentals.**

The basics, drilled over and over again, will suffice for most routine situations. Once you master the fundamentals, build on them and adapt them to more challenging circumstances. I have used all kinds of materials to stabilize limbs, and I know that any skill can be developed through practice.

It doesn't matter whether you're providing security for the Pope, the G-8 and G-20 Summits, or access control to the World Exchange Plaza. This principle applies to working at events like concerts, festivals or other major events like Canada Day activities. Whatever you do, think about the fundamentals of preparedness. You can only fulfill (and surpass) our clients' expectations and save lives **by drilling and rehearsing the fundamentals to the point that they become instinctive.**

This is just as true for our "routine" contracts as it is for the high profile assignments. You have to be as ready to deal with a heart attack as you are with giving people directions. When you scrutinize people entering a commercial building, for instance, you have to be just as diligent as you are when searching the bags of patrons coming to an NHL game. Imagine how much safer the world would be if every security officer was always conscientious.

The skills you use will vary from situation to situation, but you must first have a solid understanding of the foundations. You can't build a house if the foundation isn't secure. Just as a chameleon changes colours to fit in with its environment, so you must be able to easily adapt to new circumstances.

Security Officers' Fundamentals Include: (partial list)
1. Observing and reporting maintenance deficiencies.
2. Ensuring a safe environment for all tenants, occupants, and visitors.
3. Performing security protocols—that keep honest people honest and deter criminal activity.
4. Actively patrolling the site and communicating with internal and external customers.
5. Providing excellent customer service.

Hospitals have their own unique security needs. So do hotels. At NASS, we also provide ongoing services for high-tech companies. The security strategies they require differ markedly from those demanded of us by shopping centres. We also provide security for biotechnology corporations and pharmaceutical companies and Crown corporations. **Each of these sites has its own security protocols**, and each client demands a set of distinct security procedures. But you must apply the same fundamentals to each one of these very different locations.

Always remember and practice the basics. Build on them as each new situation dictates. And remember: Your preparedness saves lives.

Before moving on, let's return once more to the fundamentals of being prepared. By anticipating, imagining, and thinking about the situations that could come up at work, and how you would respond to them, you can take the appropriate steps to prepare yourselves for the inevitable day when such a situation emerges. In addition, by drilling and rehearsing the fundamentals to the point that they become instinctive, you can prepare yourselves to act quickly and without hesitation in an emergency.

Now let's turn to another crucial trait that we security officers must cultivate in ourselves: curiosity.

Curiosity

When Eric and I were climbing down the scree slope during the first day of our hike, I started to sense that something was wrong. The horizon didn't look quite right. Because I am curious by nature, I am a keen observer. And in this instance, my powers of observation undoubtedly saved our lives. I do not want to imagine what might have happened had I not been alert to, and aware of our surroundings.

Security officers tend to be very curious people. We take nothing for granted. Someone who was authorized to enter a building yesterday might not be authorized to enter it today. We are the kind of people who **investigate** a small rock left by a perimeter door because we suspect that this may permit someone to block its proper functioning. We **examine** things that are out of place, out of order, and not in sync with the site protocol. By challenging and questioning everything, we help prevent disaster. **By applying the principle of curiosity to our work and to our lives, we help ensure the safety of others as well as our own.**

Curiosity needs to be tempered by good judgment. Being a good judge means being able to think about the consequences of your actions before you carry them out. In other words, by imagining and being curious about the results of an action before you perform it, you can judge whether the action is appropriate.

Imagine the following: You are working at a shopping mall and you observe an individual who is wearing a large trench coat despite the fact that it is a summer's day. What would you do? After all, the guy could just be feverish and feeling cold (in which case, you might wonder what he is doing in a shopping mall in the first place!). Or the guy could be carrying a weapon underneath the coat. Or perhaps he feels embarrassed by the clothes he's wearing. You do not want to jump to conclusions; he might have a perfectly innocent reason for wearing a coat. After observing this person for some time, you and your colleague might decide to approach him. If you do so, you might choose to call for backup.

You must mentally prepare for these situations, and you can do so in your quieter moments. **Envisioning all possible scenarios and being curious about everything that draws your attention will prepare you for crises.**

Tip 1: A good practice is to always look at the palms of people's hands. If you observe their palms, you will be more likely to detect a weapon.

Tip 2: If you are approaching someone who might become violent, you are far better off calling for backup and working together to contain the suspect. Approaching a suspect with at least one other person ensures that he is far less likely to become confrontational. One of the biggest strengths of a police officer is his ability to call for backup. There is strength in numbers. Therefore, if you're working alone, a common situation in our industry, observe the suspect from a distance. If you decide to approach him, call building operations for support. If they can't help, ask your control centre to send a mobile patrol. If they can't do that, call the civic authorities. Don't try to be a hero and go at it alone; it will be too late to think of calling for backup once you're lying on the ground. By observing from a distance and reporting what you're seeing—by being curious—you're actually being "heroic" in the performance of your duties.

"At NASS, we have an excellent training program, but each of us learns differently. Each security officer has the responsibility to make sure that he or she finds the answers to all their questions. Never be afraid to ask. There's nothing wrong with it. In fact, the opposite is true. If you see a closed door, ask what lies behind it. We make our jobs much more interesting by asking why we're doing a patrol. We can't use hardware unless we know how. If we don't know how to use a special piece of emergency equipment-like an Evac Chair, for instance, we ask. That way, we become capable of dealing with the problems that arise at the sites.

Recently, I started to learn about the importance of curiosity from an unexpected teacher: my three-year old daughter, Tara. She never stops asking why. If I'm driving to work, she asks why we're in the car. "I have to go to work." "Why," she demands. "Because I need to make a living." "Why," she asks again. "Because I need to buy food for us." "Why" "To feed you." "Oh." Tara doesn't stop asking until she gets to the bottom of her question, until she gets an answer that satisfies her. As people in the security industry, we should also ask why in regards to everything in our environment. Just as Tara, my "why-girl", feels that it's her job to ask questions about everything that she sees, and in that way she gains a good understanding of the world, so security officers gain a good understanding of their environment by asking why. Don't be afraid to ask. It's your duty to ask why you're doing a lock-up, to know the purpose behind everything, and to look behind every closed door.

Finally, being curious is connected to taking initiative. If you're not satisfied with your current duties, and you want to take on more challenges, show initiative. Offer to review the site orders. After my first year as a security officer with NASS, I needed greater challenges. I needed something different. So I let my supervisor know. It so happened that the control centre needed a replacement and, because I had given 100 percent throughout the year and shown my drive and dedication, I got promoted.

Remember to always ask the five Ws and How—why, where, when, who, what, and how. It'll help you to grow."

Kathleen Nolan, Vice President, NASS

Curiosity involves developing strong observation skills. Being curious means being unafraid to ask questions and being super-attentive to details and changes in our environment. Which brings us to my next pearl of wisdom: Overload.

Overload *(Positive Pressure – Not Negative Stress)*

"For me the path to success was never about attaining incredible wealth or celebrity. It was about the process of continually seeking to become better, to challenge myself to pursue excellence on every level. The question I ask myself every day is the same it's always been: How much further can I stretch to reach my fullest potential?"

Oprah Winfrey

The morning after we spent that long night trapped on the mountain, Eric was so exhausted that he couldn't take another step. Just as he had used his mental strength the day before to help me, I used my mental resilience on the second day to assist him. Since the task of climbing to the peak of the mountain seemed overwhelming, we set ourselves a very small initial goal: we began by taking five steps. Pushing ourselves to take five steps led us to eventually take 15 steps. Once we were moving, it was easier to keep moving. In other words, we developed momentum. To grow as individuals—in our lives and in our work—we must constantly seek out opportunities to challenge ourselves. On the mountain, the first five steps felt impossible, but we pushed ourselves to take them. **By pushing ourselves—by taking on more than we felt we could easily accomplish**—we were eventually able to take more and more steps without stopping.

I want to distinguish between **positive pressure** and **negative stress**. Positive pressure involves voluntarily overloading by choosing to push yourself beyond your comfort zone. If your job is too easy, two things will happen. You will quickly lose interest, and you will begin to perform poorly. By continuously pushing yourself beyond your comfort zone, you will become even better at what you do. **When we overload ourselves, the impossible becomes possible, and through repetition, the possible becomes second nature.** When taking 12 steps at a time begins to feel easy, challenge yourselves to take 15 steps. By continuously overloading yourselves, you can reach the mountain-peak of your profession.

Challenging ourselves beyond our comfort zone, or putting positive pressure on ourselves, is very different from **negative stress**. Negative stress manifests itself in exhaustion and ill health. This occurs when we do not include rest periods between periods of work. In terms of the mountain story, negative stress occurs when we do not give ourselves those two-minute breathing stops to recover. Just as the momentum of the climb increased over time, making me want to shorten the length of my rest periods, so the momentum of your work will inspire you to distribute your rest and work periods over time. **Once you get involved in the rhythm of a particular task, you will find that you have to expend less energy to complete it, allowing you to do more and more in any given day.** Although we should try to overload ourselves so as to grow as individuals, remaining healthy and energetic are key priorities. Resting is crucial.

During our hike, Eric and I continued to overload ourselves because we wanted to return safely. We overloaded ourselves in accordance with the prevailing conditions and our limitations at the time. On any other day we could have hiked for miles, but on this day, on that scree slope with loose rocks, 15 steps was overloading.

In today's world, things move ever more quickly. Before 1986, cell phones—or hip-phones as I like to call them—did not exist. Today, they have transformed the pace and the quality of our communication. Now we even have hip E-mail (such as Blackberries and Palms). We are expected to communicate more and more efficiently.

Overloading ourselves becomes crucial not only to growing as individuals, but to remaining competitive in our industry. At NASS– and I know it's the same at most companies– the best candidates for promotion are the ones who maximize their time and apply themselves fully to every task at hand. By doing so, they advance in the company and grow as individuals. NASS is a very innovative company in the security business because it—meaning its *people*—continually overload themselves. We challenge ourselves to improve in a consistent, methodical manner.

By overloading ourselves, we grow.

Now that we understand the importance of overloading ourselves, let's discuss another tactic to deal with challenges: resilience.

Resilience

In the security business, tasks can sometimes appear so large that they seem impossible to complete. We don't even know where to begin. On the morning following our seemingly endless night on the mountain, Eric felt that reaching the mountain's peak was an impossible task. **By breaking the challenge of climbing the mountain into smaller, attainable goals, we eventually made it to the top.** From that experience, I learned to fulfill a task by mentally separating the task into chunks, slices or slivers.

As security officers, you often have to patrol very large complexes. How do you cover a large area within the time requirements? You use the principle I've just described. You break down the patrol into interior floor-by-floor patrols, retail patrols, parking lot patrols, mechanical equipment room patrols, external perimeter patrols, etc. In this way, you make what seems like an impossibly large task into something manageable.

Remember to break down a large task or a series of tasks into slivers, slices, and chunks. Dedicate yourself to a sliver at a time, and soon you will find that a slice of the task has been completed. Take on the next slice, and soon you will find that a chunk of the task is done.

I've saved my best tactic for last. By being prepared, curious, overloading and resilient—by applying the above four traits—you will be ready to use the fifth one.

Purpose

"The purpose of human life is to serve and to show compassion and the will to help others."
                    Albert Schweitzer, Nobel Peace Prize winner, 1952

Just as the "true mountain guy" was the expert on the mountain, so we security officers are the experts on our sites. Just as the mountain guy used his expertise to help Eric and I reach the bottom of the mountain safely, so you use your expertise in providing security and excellent customer service to help others. **Helping others is the most important aspect of living.** This is the greatest lesson I have learned in my life. Enjoying yourself and seeking knowledge are also important aspects of life. But nothing is as fulfilling as helping others. Helping others gives our lives meaning.

This is the fundamental concept behind the hiring choices we make at NASS. When we hire security personnel, the key question we ask is whether they want to be of service to others. A person might be a great technician, excellent at self-defense, or super-knowledgeable about computers, but we will not hire him or her if they do not demonstrate a commitment to helping others.

Just as Eric and I still remember the mountain-guy and his willingness to help us, **your service to others greatly affects their lives**. For the man who helped us, hiking up the mountain was routine. So helping us came as second nature to him and he did it without panic or hesitation. He knew the mountain so well that getting us to the bottom was a comparatively easy task. You could say that it was "all in a day's work" for him, but his actions saved our lives. Some day, while you are doing a "routine" patrol, you could come across a security breach, a fire, or a safety hazard—you will shine. **When you are fully engaged in your tasks, it's easy to be heroic when a crisis arises.**

Summary

1. **Preparedness**: Being prepared comes from thinking about all the things that could possibly happen during your shift.
2. **Curiosity**: Be curious about, and question, things that seem out of place.
3. **Overload**: Push yourself to give your all.
4. **Resilience**: Break the work into chunks, slices, and slivers and move through them systematically.
5. **Purpose**: Never forget to look at the bigger picture.

Boma Award - Above and Beyond

Security is like insurance- you strongly hope you never have to use it- but if you do, you are extremely glad it's there.

Such was the case at a multi-use commercial facility in downtown Ottawa where North American Security Services (NASS) guards came face to face with a man, armed with a large knife, demanding money from tenants. Their actions to protect the employees from the perpetrator led to NASS receiving the 1996 BOMA Canada Pinnacle Award for service above and beyond the call of duty.

Ottawa Police were called to the scene at the building where a 23-year-old man entered the Bank of Montreal management offices located on the 8th floor at 8:30 a.m. mistaking the offices for a banking facility. The suspect entered the office area demanding money from three employees who were personally robbed of an undisclosed amount of personal cash. Inside the office area, a Bank of Montreal employee had an altercation with the suspect and suffered several stab wounds to the upper body and was taken by ambulance to the Ottawa Hospital.

A building spokesperson says the extent of the employee's injuries were quite severe and included a damaged carotid artery, punctured lungs, kidney laceration, severed jugular vein, severed fingertips (one was lost and two were later reattached in an operation at the hospital), paralysis to the entire upper left quadrant of the shoulder and head, slashed palms, five stab wounds to the

back, two stab wounds to the side and one stab wound to the face. He was on life support at the hospital for three days.

The suspect was confronted by two NASS security guards in the hallway. The guards attempted to calm the suspect and offered to help him get to the ground floor. The guards alerted another guard on the main floor. Three police patrol officers and a building security guard met the suspect as he came off an elevator onto the main floor. The suspect threw his knife in the direction of two police officers and was tackled by the third police officer.

After getting the suspect into the elevator the security guards immediately returned to the victim and applied first aid and are attributed for helping save the victim's life.

"Safety is a matter of being prepared," states a spokesman for NASS. "Once you are prepared, you can take action quickly and without hesitation. Also, panic is less likely to occur."

Chapter Three

Principles That Help Us Serve Others Better

"Think enthusiastically about everything, especially about your job. If you do so, you'll put a touch of glory in your life."

Norman Vincent Peale, U.S. clergyman and writer

In the service industry, providing quality service is its own reward. The key is making quality service easy to provide. At NASS, we have implemented a number of protocols that, when followed, improve the quality of service we provide to our customers. Here are a few of them.

The IGA Example

This is one of NASS' founding principles. Its name was inspired by the high quality of customer service we saw in the early 1980's at the IGA grocery stores. We noticed that the IGA staff arrived at work at least 15 minutes before their shifts began. That way, they had enough time to drink a coffee, chat with their colleagues, and change into their uniforms. When IGA opens its doors to the public, the cashiers are ready at their posts to serve the first customer, having counted and prepared the till. Because the cashier arrives at least 15 minutes early, the moment the shift begins, he or she is fully prepared to offer excellent customer service. At NASS, we incorporated this principle into the work practices of our security officers, supervisors, and executives.

There are many important reasons why you should all arrive at work *at least* 15 minutes before your shifts begin:

Imagine that you work the midnight to 8 a.m. shift. By the time 8 a.m. rolls around, all you want to do is go home. You want to leave right away. Now imagine that your shift replacement strolls in at 7:55 a.m. He or she hasn't changed into uniform, hasn't had a morning coffee, and wants to talk about last night's football game. You can't wait to leave, but now you may have to wait another 15 minutes while your replacement gets his or her act together. What's

more, you have a number of pass-ons to give. How do you feel?
Less than impressed, I bet.

It is more than likely that you will always want to leave
right at the end of your shift. Everyone has things they want to do
outside of their work. Just as you expect your shift replacement to
respect you by arriving at work at least 15 minutes before the
changeover—so you should show respect for your peers by showing
up early, too, and giving yourself enough time to get into work-
mode. When your shift begins, you must be in uniform, fully
prepared and alert.

In other companies, some security officers have not been
willing to arrive to work 15 minutes early. I suppose they come to
work already in full uniform, having had their coffee, and lacking
any desire to socialize. All of us, including managers and
supervisors, need **transition** time. We all need at least 15 minutes to
switch mental gears.

At NASS, we take measures to protect all our security
officers. If someone is late for their shift, causing their colleague to
stay longer, the person who is late loses the corresponding amount
from their wage. If your colleague is late and you have to work part
of their shift, you will be compensated for your extra time. But I
imagine you would still feel unhappy about having to work longer
than you expected, if you had plans—dinner with a friend, picking
up the car at the garage, a movie, an early bedtime— for the time
after your shift. Similarly, if *you* are 30 minutes late, the equivalent
amount will be deducted from *your* wage. Unreliability has an
adverse effect on everyone, and you may be subject to disciplinary
action.

In business, we often refer to Murphy's Law: If something
can go wrong, it *will* go wrong. In other words, always expect the
unexpected. We can be sure that when an emergency arises, it will
arise during a shift change. It is during these transition periods,
opening and closing, and during handovers, that people are the least
alert. During these times employees often think that their outgoing
colleague is still responsible for the site. But it's precisely during
these times that people need to be extra-vigilant.

Imagine this scenario: a criminal decides to rob a jewelry store. He will do it during the opening or closing moments, because this is when the store is most **vulnerable**—all the cash and all the jewelry are in one place. So, it's during these transition times that we need to pay extra attention to details and follow our protocols.

During handovers from one shift to another, security officers often let their guard down. **It's at the moment of the handshake that both security officers should be most attentive.** If an emergency occurs one minute before the beginning of your shift, who is responsible for dealing with it? If your shift begins at 4 p.m., Murphy's Law guarantees that an emergency will occur at 3:59 p.m., in which case you will have to be ready to deal with it. If you arrive at work at 3:59 p.m. and you're not in uniform and you're still thinking about last night's hockey game, you will not be prepared to deal with the situation. It's another good reason why coming to work 15 minutes early is so important. When your shift begins, it is your responsibility to cope with any problem that crops up. You had better be ready for it. And if you come in 15 minutes early, you will be.

Just like the IGA example, the principle of **Follow up and Closure** shows our peers, supervisors, and customers that we are reliable people.

> *"From my own experience I have come to believe that what you put into a job is what you get out of it. Staff members who give their all to the job will derive greater job satisfaction. And what's more, the satisfied staff member—the one who puts his all into the job—is the one who will get noticed and will move more quickly up the company's ranks. The security officer who works hard, shows an interest, cares about his or her work, is the one who will find him or herself in the control centre or in the rank of a manager."*
>
> *Dana Fleming, Leadership Team, NASS*

The Principle of Follow-Up and Closure

Consistently following up on each task makes for a strong manager and a top-notch security officer. We often have to multi-task. It's very easy to forget to follow up on every one of these tasks. It's easy to miss something. But during the quieter moments, we can ask ourselves "Did I look at everything? Did I follow-up with the tenant who asked about the windows?"

While on patrol, you may notice items that need to be fixed. A loose handrail might give way and cause someone to fall. A burnt-out light provides a cloak of darkness that could invite criminal behavior. It's not enough to mechanically record your observations and to assume that the proper authority will remedy the situation. As security officers, we must realize that only when the item is fixed, can the maintenance issue be closed.

It is our responsibility to report closure on the item. A valuable feature of NASS' on-line reporting system (to be discussed in a later chapter) is that it allows upper management to easily track maintenance deficiencies and other matters through security officers' updated reports. Your supervisor will ask for feedback on the status of the task. You must notify everyone concerned that the task has been completed. If the completion is delayed or impossible to achieve, you must provide that information as well.

"Owning" every single one of your tasks, large and small, will help you get the most out of your job. By following up and giving closure to every task, you will feel a sense of accomplishment. You will become outstanding security officers and expert customer service agents.

Just as following-up and giving closure to your tasks guarantees your reliability, so understanding the principle of under-promising and over-delivering will ensure that your customers are happy and cooperative.

The Principle of Under-Promising and Over-Delivering

Imagine the following scenario: a customer calls and asks for something. You promise that you will call back with the information in the next 10 minutes. You call back 12 minutes later. Although you're only two minutes late, in the customer's eyes you have failed to fulfill your promise. As soon as you told them you would call back in 10 minutes, you created an expectation. By calling 12 minutes later you over-promised and under-delivered. To be the best security officers you can be you do the opposite. **We must under-promise and we over-deliver**.

Let's consider the scenario again: the customer calls and asks for something. You promise that you will call them back with the needed information in no more than 15 minutes. You call them back *12 minutes* later. In the customer's eyes, you have done an excellent job; in fact, you have surpassed their expectations and saved them time. You under-promised; and you over-delivered. The result: a happy customer. Happy customers are more likely to give positive feedback to upper management about the value of your services.

> *"Morguard currently manages 36.5 million square feet of space, valued in excess of $3.4 billion. Many of the buildings are protected by on-site security officers who have the massive responsibility of watching over multi-million dollar assets, while we are all at home sleeping. It is a service which is, and will become, more crucial in our society. The security industry is growing in importance, especially with the increase in terrorist activity in the world. I personally believe the benefits and salaries of the security officer will improve over time. Morguard has been proactive in establishing higher minimum pay rates and benefits within our current documents.*
>
> *Property managers, such as me, are members of the service industry. We must provide a safe, comfortable, and convenient environment for our tenants. Security personnel are an extension of us. We all work together towards a common goal, to provide excellent service.*
>
> *My favorite proverb, which comes from the book of Proverbs in the Bible (11: 25) is: "He that watereth shall be watered himself." I have tried to live by that philosophy in work and in play, and I certainly have lots for which to be thankful."*
>
> *Steve Hebert, Property Manager, Morguard Investments*

Root Cause Analysis

In the past decade, I've seen property owners and managers respond to increased security concerns and incidents by adding card readers to their card access systems, or a camera to their closed-circuit television system (CCTV). Sometimes, they respond to problems by requesting another security officer on the site. These are all good ways to improve overall security. However, if a true **root cause analysis** is completed, you will often find that improved processes and procedures can often be more effective at resolving a specific problem.

Avoid Band-aid solutions—cosmetic fixes that hide the real problem! A security officer must strive to find the root cause of a problem before trying to fix it. NASS takes pride in its tremendous ability to perform root causes analysis.

Let's look at three illustrations. Let's say there has been an increase in laptop thefts in an office tower. One response could be to hire an extra security officer per shift. This could work well, as the presence of another security officer acts as a deterrent. As well, another officer on site means more personnel will be around to respond to emergencies. However, in this situation, before adding an extra security officer per shift, NASS would perform a root cause analysis. NASS' **Virtual Private Network (VPN)** enables us to identify the reported time of the thefts. We then do a trend analysis. We run reports to reveal the number of visitors coming through access control points throughout the day. This time analysis shows that the volume of visitors increases between the hours of 3 p.m. and 7 p.m. This finding justifies putting two additional security officers on during this time, whereas no additional personnel may be required between 7 p.m. and 11 p.m. An increase in personnel during the office tower's busiest hours enhances our access management, which in turn increases the chances that we will notice suspicious behaviour.

In this situation, however, NASS would go even further to identify the root cause. We would measure the frequency rate of visitors against the dates and times of the reported thefts. Root cause analysis may reveal that the owner of the office tower would benefit more from extra personnel during high volume hours than by adding additional cameras and card readers to entry and exit systems. Again, although installing more hardware would improve the site's overall security, the new technology would not target the specific problem.

Okay, let's consider another example. At a particular site, tenants complain that they don't see the security officers. The complaint seems bizarre because security patrols the site 24/7. Before responding to the complaint by adding additional staff, we should ask some probing questions. Perhaps one of the security officers doesn't greet the tenants, and the lack of eye-contact makes some tenants feel as though the building lacks security personnel. Or perhaps it's an ergonomic problem. The style of the lobby's reception desk makes it necessary for the security officer to look down to monitor the computer screens. To solve the problem, we may have to redesign the work station. We want the officer to be able to sit comfortably and monitor the screens, as well as easily interact with tenants as they pass by. Perhaps we can accommodate the tenants' desire to feel acknowledged by adjusting the height of the desk and the chair.

Perhaps the issue of visibility is not related to the height of the desk, but to its location. Maybe the lobby needs better lighting, especially around the reception desk. We may have to increase signage around the desk. Or, the problem may lie in the fact that the security officer's uniform is not distinctive enough. If security officers blend in—because they dress like the clerks who work in the building—guests may not easily distinguish the security staff from office workers, and conclude that the building has no security officers. By probing into the complaint of security visibility, we can identify the real issue and respond appropriately.

As security officers, your reports are crucial to this solution process. If you report that a door was unlocked at 3:30 p.m. on the Tuesday of one week, the Thursday of the next, and the Wednesday of the third, there may be a common thread. It may be that a cleaner worked during all those shifts and left the doors open. Rather than assume that the unlocked door was evidence of a security breach, root-cause analysis may reveal that it was carelessness or poor training on the part of one of the cleaners.

31

Now let's take this example further: You notice that maintenance staff have to keep fixing the same broken doorknob. You point this out to your manager, who examines the building's data and notices that this door is the only one in the building with this recurring problem. Based on the information in your reports, your supervisor concludes that faulty hardware is not the problem, because all the building's doors are the same and no other knobs need repair. This isolated case could be related to wear and tear on the door because of the high volume or the problem could be caused by run-off from an overhead eaves trough that's ruining the knob's seal.

The temporary solution—changing the door handle again and again—does not eliminate the real problem. Root cause analysis reveals that the equipment may need to be changed. Now you can make some educated suggestions.

As security officers, you must not think that it's only your supervisors' and clients' responsibility to come up with solutions to problems at your site. You can provide crucial assistance by dealing with problems that jeopardize the safety of your working environment. After all, that is your responsibility.

Let's consider a more serious variation on the above example: the door may only appear to have been broken. Perhaps a person was attempting to illegally enter the building by putting paper in the latch to make the door seem locked. This can be discovered through a root cause analysis. With the help of such an analysis, you can prevent an illegal entry.

Identifying the root cause of a problem is one of the best ways to provide excellent security and customer service to your clients.

One last note: sometimes supervisors and clients may be slow to respond to your findings. This does not mean that your reports have been ignored. It may simply mean that the supervisors are evaluating the situation to find objective, empirical evidence on the problem, and brainstorming an effective solution to it.

Living with Purpose

"The average person puts only 25 percent of his energy and ability into his work. The world takes off its hat to those who put in more than 50 percent of their capacity, and stands on its head for those few and far between souls who devote 100 percent."
                    Andrew Carnegie, industrialist and philanthropist

To live with purpose, you have to understand how your work benefits other people. The mountain-guy sure understood this, and we tipped our hats off to him. When you live with purpose, you approach your work—and all aspects of your life—with energy and passion. We get from life and from our jobs what we put into them.

Most people dread Monday mornings. And when the whistle blows on Friday afternoon, they take their money and run. Because they don't see how their work has meaning, they don't produce meaningful results. They meet the minimum requirements, and in turn they probably complain about their jobs. If they view each stroke of the clock as a sign of a few more dollars, and their paycheck as the means to acquire the real pleasures of life, then they can't wait for those 40 hours a week to be over and that paycheck to arrive.

Life isn't a dress rehearsal for the real thing. This is it. Life is now. A 40-hour workweek is a huge chunk of time—don't waste it.

Live time; don't kill time!

NASS takes pride in its success. Employees who joined the company at the entry level a few years ago now have roles on its leadership team. Some of our entry-level employees have become managers at public security agencies such as the RCMP, OPP, city police etc. Still others have become lawyers in the Justice Department.

Some people believe they are restricted as to how far they can go in their careers. But these people have set their own limits.

Customers feel the striking contrast between a security officer who smiles and offers a helping hand, and one who huffs and puffs over every minor hassle. The first kind of security officer understands what it means to live with purpose. He knows that being of service to others can be one of life's pleasures and will no doubt enjoy the rewards of our profession and advance quickly. The second kind of security officer will quickly see that his misery, experienced at work (because of attitude), penetrates other areas of his life. By changing his approach to work, he may also enjoy the positive spillover effects in other areas of his life.

When we live with purpose and enjoy our work, the size of our paycheck becomes less of an issue. I've seen those miserable folks who reluctantly drag themselves into work eventually make less than those who approach their work with passion.

To conclude: the principles we've discussed will help us all become even better security officers. By being ready to start at the start of our shifts, incorporating the rules of follow-up and closure, under-promising and over-delivering, and employing root cause analysis, we will provide premium service to our customers and understand the purpose of our work.

Chapter Four
Customer Service

"The people to whom we give, may or may not show gratitude, but [each act of service] we extend strengthens the pillars of the world."

Maya Angelou, writer and activist

Four Steps to Excellent Service

1. **Empathy**
   Understand the client's point of view
   Determine each customer's unique needs
2. **Individual Responsibility**
   Anticipate needs and exceed expectations
   Follow up to ensure total satisfaction
3. **Making It Personal**
   Refer to each client by name
   Make each customer feel welcome (as if you
   were the host/hostess in your own home)
4. **Courtesy**
   Use professional etiquette
   Show appreciation
   Always be courteous

Remember: Be an ambassador for your site.

Customer Service and What It Means to "Sell"

When someone says "I'm in sales," it often conjures up something vaguely sleazy – perhaps the image of a deceitful used-car salesman. Selling in our culture has negative associations and I think that is very unfortunate. I'll tell you why. Because, ultimately, everyone in the world is "in sales." We all "sell" to each other in some way. As security officers—experts in customer services—we're salespeople. By doing our jobs effectively, we sell the importance of our job functions. People think badly about the job of selling a used car. But why should they? If you sell a used car in an honest way, why should you be ashamed? After all, you're fulfilling a need: some people want a used car. Obviously you shouldn't try to pretend it's a new car, but you can certainly play up its good points: for example, the fact that it's only been driven for a year and a half and it has low mileage. You can emphasize the positive without denying the negative.

Let's consider the following example from our work: Some people see access control as a barrier that prevents them from entering the building as quickly as they would like. We, as security officers, should sell our protocols by explaining to our customers the advantages of implementing access control procedures. We should help people see access control for what it is: a necessary process that facilitates access to authorized people and protects the assets and interest of the company. Among other things, it cuts down on theft and keeps everybody safer. In addition, access control ensures that, in the event of an emergency, we know who is in the building.

Although this protocol may not seem relevant on a routine day, its importance is highlighted when a thief attempts a security breach. If someone enters a building five times a day, they might not see the need to show their badge each time. But as Erin Lang, of NASS' Leadership Team, says, "We sell our protocols by explaining why they must show their badge each and every time they enter the building. Part of customer service and sales involves educating people as to why the functions we provide are crucial to ensuring their safety and the site's integrity." In other words, we sell the benefits of our service.

You "sell" your competence and your caring attitude to your customers. You also "sell" them the site protocols. You sell the positive aspects of what you do.

At NASS, many of our security officers hold indoor patrol and desk positions in Class "A" office complexes located in major cities. Most of the occupants of these buildings are people with good values who have a great respect for security. NASS security officers gain a sense of dignity from being of service to people who respect them and rely on their presence. And we work under pleasant conditions in environmentally-controlled buildings that are clean and comfortable.

By contrast, working outdoors can be very demanding. Imagine being part of a road crew pouring hot asphalt in the blistering heat, or salting roads in a snowstorm, or holding a traffic sign in the pouring rain. It makes you appreciate your workplace, doesn't it? A nice modern office is a great environment in which to spend an eight-hour shift.

Did you notice what I was just doing? I was "selling" you on some of the benefits of your job. Similarly, you must sell the benefits of site protocols to your customers by educating them as to why we do what we do.

Who Is Our Customer? What Can We Do for Them?

"When we shop for new running shoes, or dine out with friends, we appreciate good service and product value. When the service and value are less than we expected, we react in a variety of ways. We may decide not to give that establishment any repeat business and tell many of our friends and family of the negative experience we had. We also can develop a negative connection between the product and the service, even though we may have been dissatisfied with only one aspect. If you buy a sweater from a store and the colours fade when you wash it, for example, you may think of the store as a place that sells cheap clothing. If the store can win back your confidence through positive customer recovery (making you happy again), the likelihood that you will return and give praise increases.

How do you, as a security professional, have an impact on customers who frequent your facility, and more so, who are your customers? Does your definition of a customer change because you work at an industrial facility as opposed to a tourist destination? Is your partner, who's calling in a patrol, your customer? Is the person who tells you about the burnt-out light in the hallway your customer? The answer is clear: Regardless of our venue, everyone we deal with is a customer: They all deserve the same high level of service that you expect. Have you ever thought of the contractor signing in as your customer? What impact do you have when it comes to representing yourself and the company? Your actions, attitudes and behaviour reflect not only upon yourself, but the companies that you represent. Companies? Yes, not only the company that you work for directly, but also the companies who own or manage property, and the tenants of space within your site. Unfortunately, stereotyping occurs when people associate the actions of one with the group as a whole. If you receive poor service from one waiter at a restaurant, you may think of the establishment as a bad restaurant. Fact is, that it was only the one waiter who caused you to form that negative opinion. If your customers receive the same poor service that you received from the waiter, they will form the same negative opinion of you and your company that you formed of the waiter and his restaurant.

It is vital that you are able to recognize who your customer is, and what you need to do to ensure they remain your customer and not someone else's."

Patrick Ogilvie, Chief of Security, CN Tower.

**An Illustration of Premium Customer Service:
The Customer Drives the Business**

July 30th 2002:

Last Friday in the early morning, there was an electrical fire at NASS' dry cleaners. The owner was in England at the time. NASS monitors the burglar system. There was no smoke or heat detector in the store. All that was left of the store was the shell of the building, a cinderblock structure. All the clothes were destroyed and the cash register gone.

I was away over the weekend. On Monday morning, I went by the drycleaners to drop something off. When I arrived at the store, I could smell the smoke damage although the fire had occurred four days earlier. To my disbelief, **it was business as usual**. "WE ARE OPEN," read the sign on the door. "SEE ATTENDANT IN THE WHITE VAN PARKED IN FRONT OF THE STORE."

Just as the sign said, inside the minivan sat the regular clerk taking orders, receiving clothes and handing out cleaned clothes. The glove box in the van was now the new cash register. They had made arrangements for another dry cleaner to clean the clothes, and the minivan has become a drop off center with a one day turnaround. I kid you not. They did not want to lose their client base. **The customer drives the business**.

I have always respected the owner of the store. I now respect him even more!

Your Impact

As security officers we are very fortunate: we get to interact with people a lot. We have a chance to make an impression on others. If, for instance, you are working in a building all by yourself at two in the morning, the effect you have on the people who come by is enormous. The smile you give them, the polite manner with which you greet them, can have a tremendous impact. You might be the only person they see that entire evening and because of this, your effect on them is greatly magnified.

The quality of the effect you have is up to you. You can choose to have a positive or a negative impact. For example, imagine that you have to deal with a guy delivering a package. He's grumpy. Perhaps he didn't want to be working at this hour when he could be out with friends. Your friendly, energetic approach to him will make him feel that things aren't so bad.

High-level executives and dedicated employees also stop by their office buildings during the quiet hours. It feels good to be recognized as a hard worker by these people, who may have also worked their way up from entry-level positions. High-level executives respect security officers who approach their job seriously. At two a.m., we have the gift of time, and in a one-on-one situation, the opportunity to make a favourable impression. Use your tools: your smile, your tall stance, and your professional demeanor to lift the spirit of another dedicated worker.

It's a challenge to keep your standards high during the quiet times. During the overnight shift, you are more likely to let down your guard. These are the moments, however, when you should make even more of an effort to stay alert. You must be professional at all times.

It can be difficult to see the benefits of providing security services at two a.m. when there's nobody around. You may think: what's the harm in relaxing? But the occupants of the building don't see it that way. It is very important to them that you stay on the ball, no matter what time it is. They trust that you will protect their belongings at all hours, and especially in their absence (and during their sleep). They pay us to protect them, so that they can let *their* guard down.

On the other hand, you may work at a busy post during regular office hours, interacting with many people, Monday through Friday. That situation can have its temptations as well. Seeing a lot of people can lead to laxity. You might start to overlook the importance of taking the time to be polite and thorough. If you're very busy, and people are throwing punches at you all day long—figuratively speaking—you have to be able to re-direct your energy quickly. In other words, you cannot lose your professional disposition even when your environment becomes familiar.

"The more professional and sincere our front-line staff are, the more confident our patrons and tenants will be. Excellent security in the form of people and programs coupled with superior customer services will have a positive influence on our relationships with our clients.

We ensure our front-line staff are trained in the art and importance of providing exceptional customer service, by ensuring all have the benefit of our on-going "World-Class Service Training." People look to the staff's uniforms and rely on their knowledge, particularly when it comes to security. During a fire alarm or other perceived emergency, building occupants rely and depend on the security officer's training, experience and professionalism. If security officers appear flustered, panicked or unsure of themselves or the procedures, those observing will also be anxious when taking directions or instructions from them. However, if the security officers are poised and confident, patrons will be more confident that the situation is under control and anxieties will be minimized.

Stereotypes about security personnel are the result of the lack of professionalism of a few. A career-minded security officer who approaches patrons with courtesy and a smile challenges those negative stereotypes.

We share our buildings and our city with many people. By being courteous and professional, your job will not only be easier, it will be more enjoyable. "

Glenn N. Thornley, RPA Director, Oxford Properties Group

At a concert, for instance, 20 people might ask you how to find the washroom in a span of about 10 minutes. By the time the 20th person asks the question, you might be fed up answering it, and that might prompt an impatient reply. Your professionalism is slipping. What you have to remember is that those 20 people are all individuals, and each one of them approached you because they saw you as the on-site expert. They look to you for help. Just as the mountain guy was the expert of the mountain, you're the experts during the concert. You have the knowledge to help others. And just as the mountain guy helped us without hesitation, we too should serve our customers with a positive, "can-do" attitude.

Just as you drill for emergencies—in case, for example, someone has a heart attack during a concert, and you have to get him or her to the hospital as quickly and as discreetly as possible—you also drill for the more routine possibilities: a sprained wrist, a bad cut, an allergic reaction, a broken ankle, etc. When any of these things occur, you're onstage. So you must be prepared to act quickly and without hesitation. Your goal will be to keep the other concert-goers calm and to allow the performance to continue while you attend to the injured guest.

Although there is a *probability* that at a concert of 50,000 people, you will have to provide some form of medical attention, it is a *certainty* that at a concert of 50,000 people, you will have to direct many guests to the washroom, to the confection stands, etc. You have to be equally prepared for both extremes. Sometimes we minimize the importance of training for the more routine situations. **But since these situations will certainly occur, we must be ready to deal with them, and in a professional manner.** Our professional attitude greatly affects the quality of people's experiences.

In large office towers, multi-use complexes and campuses, you should also drill (mentally) for every question and every situation. When you're working at a busy post, certain questions will become routine. You always need to be aware of your tone, your posture, and your facial expressions. If you are aware of how you are coming across, you can accentuate your impact on the people you encounter. If you have the right kind of presence, people will be more likely to cooperate when you need them to.

Think, for instance, about how you would direct a phased evacuation. As soon as people hear the fire alarm, everyone, including experienced security officers, gets anxious; your heart beats faster. You alert the areas that must evacuate immediately and the ones that must remain on stand-by. The moment you activate the public address system you are centre-stage: "Attention, Attention. We have received an alarm." How do you project your voice? The calm, confident tone is part of what our clients want and expect. If you are unprepared and you stutter while speaking on the fire-communication panel, for instance, you will have a hard time calming the occupants of the building. But if you project your words clearly and with confidence—which you can do because you have mentally rehearsed the action of announcing a fire many times—you make the occupants feel more secure. And they are more likely to cooperate when they feel well-guided. Your vocal tone can keep people from panicking.

Of course, it is impractical to practice the announcement of a fire drill on the public-address system. But you must examine the public-address system and think about what you would say if the situation occurred. We can perform our jobs effectively because we have prepared for such occurrences—by drilling, rehearsing, and thinking about the situation— many times before.

We live in a world where there are frequent practice fire drills and false alarms, especially in schools. Because of this, some people may assume that every fire alarm is a false one. This attitude concerns me because I have seen the horrific consequences of real fires. When a real fire alarm goes off, every second counts. Today, public-address systems may also be used when security personnel are dealing with an accident, a hazardous-material incident or other emergencies. Being prepared for such occurrences involves seemingly unconnected duties such as organizing your desk so that when the fire or bomb-threat occurs, you can immediately answer time-saving questions such as: "Where is the loud-speaker? Where are the keys to the fire-control room? Where is my jacket?"

Kevin Cooney, (Vice President, NASS) has said that **everything on a desk must have a home.** Nothing should be placed in the way. Your binders, for instance, should be organized in a way that allows you to react quickly and efficiently when an emergency arises. Your desk space must be organized so that you can be prepared for every situation.

How we come across to others can make a big difference in an emergency. Let's go on to examine how we can improve our body language and facial expressions to increase our impact.

The Power of a Smile

"Too often we underestimate the power of a smile, a kind word, a listening ear, an honest compliment, or the smallest act of caring, all of which have the potential to turn a life around."
                                                                    Leo Buscaglia, poet

A genuine smile is very powerful. It makes the person smiling feel more energetic. It makes the person receiving the smile feel significant and acknowledged. **A positive attitude is key to motivating ourselves and to motivating others.** When you use your enthusiasm to motivate others, they are more likely to cooperate with you, work productively and enjoy their shift.

As security officers, we can use our smiles as a tool. In the security business, I've see a smile defuse the anger of a very hostile person. Imagine: A busy executive has to stop and change a tire on his way to a business meeting. Not only has he dirtied his shirt; he has lost a lot of time, and now he is late. As he approaches the front desk, you ask him for his ID. As it happens, he has forgotten it in the car. Your request is the last straw and he flips out. Now is your chance to have a positive impact by giving him a smile. It may feel natural to respond with anger at someone who is yelling at you, especially when you're only doing your job. But if you make it second nature to respond positively and politely all the time, you can often defuse a customer's frustration. This situation is an opportunity to give someone else a lift. When the executive returns from his car with his ID, thank him with a *genuine* smile.

I have also witnessed security officers making a bad situation worse by responding aggressively to an angry guest. In this kind of scenario, the security officer escalates the guest's anger, doing both the guest and himself a disservice. Responding with anger to a hostile person is very unproductive. Consider your smile as an act of charity to a person who really needs something positive at that particular moment. **Be the bigger person.**

44

The Power of a Smile

Etienne Kerr can attribute the success of his dry-cleaning business in part to his incredible smile. Although a dentist might be able to replicate Etienne's straight teeth, he couldn't replicate Etienne's fail-safe formula for a successful business: Kerr's smile is not mechanical; it's more than skin-deep. It comes from within and it expresses his zest for life. **His smile is evidence of the joy he feels in being able to be of service to others.**

His shop lies on a busy intersection of bus routes in Ottawa's downtown core. Most of his clients rush in during their hurried breaks, zipping between the lunch counter and the office. The demands of what appears to be a stressful environment are never reflected in Etienne's attitude or in his work. He always smiles as you tell him about the stain on your jacket, the speedy service that you require, and other special requests.

Dry-cleaning is a repetitive, time-consuming job that most people regard as trivial. But with his deep-rooted smile, Etienne makes his clients' trips to the dry-cleaners a pleasure. His smile affects his customers, and as a result, the act of bringing one's clothes to the dry-cleaners becomes a treat rather than a chore. I look forward to dropping off my clothes: every time I pull up to the shop, Etienne is ready to be of service—with a huge smile on his face. Sometimes he greets me at my vehicle to exchange the fresh clothes for the soiled.

For Etienne, **success is defined as happy customers.**

From a business perspective, his friendliness and professionalism attract new clients. Current customers recommend his services to their friends. The continually increasing volume of work provides many financial rewards.

A smile has power!

> *"For every person you see without a smile, give them one of yours."*
> Fruma Appotive, *My Great Aunt*

Body Language

We communicate through our gestures and our movements. That's why we use the term "body language." Something as simple as a smile can disarm an angry person, so our body language affects others. Our body language can escalate or de-escalate a tense situation.

Poor sitting postures (while at a desk) and walking postures (while on patrol) result in injuries all too often. Also, a tall stance gives the impression of alertness. And an alert security officer is better able to spot potential hazards, and to deal with them effectively. Furthermore, a tall stance is better for your back.

Compare the image of the tall, confident security officer with that of a guy who slouches and drags his feet. The sloucher looks like he just rolled out of bed and doesn't have the energy to hold up his head. He limits his observational skills to staring at the floor. He does little to deter a possible intruder and his employers probably wonder whether he is scrutinizing people who are coming into the building.

Think Tall, Hold Yourself Tall

Not only does holding yourself tall enable you to stay alert and observe more than you do when you slouch, it also ensures greater health.

Knowing a Name = Brightening a Day

On her move-in day, the security officer of the residential complex greeted the new tenant. "Hello, Miss. Welcome." The new tenant appreciated this, because it made her feel like the building would be a good, happy, and safe place to live. Weeks passed, and every day the security officer greeted the tenant with "Hello, Miss." From time to time the officer and the tenant would have a little chat about the weather or the news headlines.

One day, when the tenant passed the desk, she heard, "Hello, Miss McDonald." That was her name. The change of address made her smile. She no longer felt like another faceless "Miss" in the building. This personalization gave Susan McDonald confidence that the security officer didn't just punch in the clock. Instead, he took time to recognize the tenants; this reassured her that he would take time to check out any strangers who might enter the building.

Had the security officer addressed Susan by her first name, it would have made her uncomfortable. Addressing her by her last name struck a perfect balance between formality, friendliness and attentiveness.

Susan was pleased by the security officer's form of address, and she praised his attentiveness to her fellow tenants, family, and friends. Such a **security officer will be considered an asset to the client, rather than an expense. The simple act of addressing the occupants of a building by their last names can justify the costs of providing security for the complex.**

Powerful Personalities

It's dangerous to be negative. It can be demoralizing to the group. A negative person can de-motivate those around them. Negative vibes spread because people are inclined to complain. The workplace can be extra-sensitive to negative attitudes, when employees feel that the only way to connect with each other is by complaining about work. Two people who have little in common may feel a false sense of connection by criticizing the latest change to a policy or by putting down a co-worker. It's easy to find commonalities by complaining about work.

A positive thinker is not a naive person who is convinced that the world is perfect. Positive thinkers change what they can, and move past the little frustrations of life. They understand that it's impossible to please everyone, including themselves, all the time. **Moods are contagious.** Positive thinkers are fun to be around, and their optimism eventually counteracts the negativity that surrounds them. A positive attitude leads to greater productivity and psychological health. Remember the old saying: "If you don't have anything good to say, don't say anything at all." Being positive means raising problems in constructive ways; it means looking for resolutions; it means approaching others and your work with openness and a willingness to help. Choose to be a positive employee.

The Gold Fish in the Bowl

Imagine the following scenario: you walk into a room and you see a gold fish bowl. If you see a school of goldfish in the bowl and all but one is black, you focus on the one that's unique. Similarly, when they walk into a lobby, people focus on the security officer. We stand out.

As a security officer in uniform, you are on stage. Your uniform commands authority. If you wear it properly, and with confidence, the public will cooperate with you. If your appearance is less than smart (greasy, messy hair or too much colorful makeup, etc) people will not take you seriously, especially during an emergency, which is precisely when you need their full cooperation. People respect the uniform; they look to the uniform for guidance.

By dressing professionally, you show others that you are serious about the work you do. The kind of people who hire us tend to think of a bad guy as someone wearing earrings, long hair, and leather. Earrings and facial jewelry do not fit with the professional image we are trying to convey. If you wear facial jewelry, please consider removing it during your shifts. The clients demand a professional, conventional, "guy-next-door" look that inspires their confidence and trust. After all, the word "uniform" suggests consistency in appearance.

Giving Our All, All the Time

Our pay rate should not determine the level of effort we put into our jobs. Security officers should give their all, all the time.

Every security officer has a reason for being a part of the company and many reasons to give his or her all. There are intrinsic (psychological and emotional) and extrinsic (financial and career advancement) rewards for giving our all, all the time.

I made about $2.50 an hour during NASS' infancy, all of which I put back into the company. Had I compared my earnings with the five-digit salaries that some of my friends were making, I likely would have thrown in the towel and ended up in a profession for which I had no passion. I stuck with it, and after many years of very hard work, we now have a successful company.

My parents used to say: "It doesn't matter what you do in this world as long as you do it to the best of your ability. Just be the best that you can be." My parents never demanded that I be the best, only the best that I could be. That mentality has served me well. I've never just put in my time or punched in the clock. I've always given my all to every task.

If you want to advance in your career, you should concentrate on demonstrating your strong work ethic to your supervisor. It's your supervisor's job to recognize such efforts. Let your supervisor know that you want to get ahead.

"At NASS you have the chance to shape your own future. When I started with the company, I was looking for more than a job. I was looking for something over which I could take ownership. I found it because I expressed my needs to my supervisors. My nature is to be introverted, so going to monthly luncheons with people I didn't know and who were older than me really helped me to grow as a person. In addition, the support of my co-workers and my coaches helped me to grow. I never would have categorized myself as a salesperson, but my managers gave me a new perception of sales and showed me how to develop an honest and personal technique that works for me. Sales are an extension of customer service and cultivating relationships with our clients increases the likelihood of getting new clients.

The confidence that I've gained at work – by knowing a topic well, through meeting new people, through overcoming challenges – pours into my life outside work. I see proof at home of the organizational skills that I've acquired at work. I've also learnt about the importance of separating work from leisure. It's crucial to take breaks. Being well-rested ensures that we will come to work with more energy and greater focus.

Being a security officer might at times make you feel distanced from the company and from others. Also, politics between co-workers and between the site and head-office can wear on you. NASS' VPN is one important way to connect with others in the company and to overcome the distance. You must never limit yourself. If you're bored, or if you don't have the tools you need, you must communicate this to your supervisor. Either communicate your ideas in shift reports or e-mail your supervisor. Communicate your needs. Empower yourself. Regardless of the position you might be in, whether in a control centre or on a site, you will always find ways to improve your job. Know that you can always do better."

Erin Lang, Leadership Team, NASS

Summary

Whether you're working at a busy or a quiet post, during the day or in the early morning, your posture and presence ensure that you make a strong impression on those you meet. In addition, a tall stance keeps you healthy and makes you better able to detect changes in your environment.

Being friendly towards others heightens your own energy, helping you to get through your shift. A genuine smile is a powerful tool. It can defuse a guest's anger and promote co-operation. Remember, too, that the way you carry yourself is a form of communication. Try not to fold your arms across your chest, or slouch, or put your hands in your pockets.

Thinking positively is a skill. It's something we train ourselves to do by consciously making a list of the things we are thankful for. And we all have things to be thankful for.
Remember to always greet guests and tenants by their last names. Your formal acknowledgement shows that you are aware of who enters the building. It makes it easier to pinpoint and scrutinize strangers. Most people value the presence of professional, respectful security officers: it makes them feel safe. Your uniform, when worn properly, gives them confidence. Over the course of your career as a security officer, however, you will probably come across people who don't initially understand the need for our protocols. Sell the benefits of your job functions to these people by explaining how our protocols help them.

Let's turn now to another, important aspect of our work that enhances the customer service we provide: **formal and personal boundaries (structures).**

Chapter Five
Strengthening Structures

"I don't think much of a man who is not wiser today than he was yesterday."

Abraham Lincoln

Key Definitions

Policy

A plan of action or guiding principle adopted by an organization that determines decisions and actions. A policy is a course of action —it is not the action itself—in the same way that a map is different from traveling. Policies are mental constructs. An example: *honesty is the best policy*. Once you believe this, once this is your policy, you act according to it—you behave honestly.

Process

A series of actions and operations that achieve an end. How the plan (the policy) will be implemented. Example: the process of obtaining a driver's license.

Procedure

A set of steps, not open to interpretation, which must be followed. A set of established methods for conducting the affairs of an organized body such as a business.

You might not believe this at first, but working within boundaries gives us strength. Boundaries enable us to excel at our jobs. They are structures that have been laid out for us by those in our profession who came before us.

Let's look at it this way. Imagine that a friend has invited you to play a round of golf. But instead of taking you to a golf course, your friend stops at a park, telling you that you will play there. "But there are no holes," you say. "Well," your friend replies, "we can hit the ball; we can practice our swings." You agree to try it. After five minutes it becomes clear to you that this form of golf is no fun. Without the holes—the goal of your shots—you're not testing yourself at your game. If you were at a proper golf course, you could challenge yourself and measure your progress. You just don't feel right practicing your swing in an environment that is not suited for the purpose.

This example shows why we need suitable frameworks in order to challenge ourselves and perform our tasks in a satisfying way. At work, the company provides appropriate boundaries that help us excel at our jobs—we call these frameworks, policies, processes, and procedures.

Let's look at another example that underscores the protection we find within structures. The St. Lawrence Seaway lies between Canada and the U.S. You navigate the Seaway using charts and a navigational buoy system. Rocks, known as shoals, lie just beneath the water's surface. If you stay within the buoy system, you're assured that you won't hit a shoal. If you navigate outside of the marked channels, however, you might run aground. There are many stories of speed boat drivers who, thinking their boats were high in the water and therefore invincible, have hit shoals, with disastrous results.

Many people who explored the Seaway region before you, when the waters were unmarked, found themselves in danger. As a service to future sailors, they mapped and marked the waterway. The buoys and charts are not arbitrary. They represent the results of years of experiences. Their purpose is to protect you.

In the same way, NASS' protocols are the product of past experiences. You can stay safe within the boundaries or frameworks that seasoned security personnel have set up for you. Our protocols assist today's staff to "navigate" more wisely (and safely) than yesterday's staff. There are good reasons for opening and closing protocols, for access control, for back-up procedures, etc. We don't implement procedures "just because." When security personnel deviate from the organization's boundaries, they risk running aground.

We also recognize that as time goes on, new hazards emerge—we hit new shoals. If you do come across a new hazard or a way to improve a process, you carefully explain this to your leadership team. The team will update and modify the existing processes.

Sometimes we confuse boundaries with restrictions and limitations. Sometimes, admittedly, boundaries do feel like barriers. Yet, it is often to our advantage to have parameters to work within. Imagine being thrown into a job without any guidance. Once boundaries are set, and rules and expectations are defined, security officers have the confidence to operate with the certainty that their actions are appropriate. Working within a framework of policies, processes, and procedures gives us strength. If we follow the processes, we can be sure of achieving consistent results. When we work within a structure, we can see things more clearly, which in turn, helps us to grow.

At NASS we have, for instance, a written policy, and a process, and a procedure to deal with sexual harassment in the workplace. These help our employees to know exactly what is permissible and what is not permissible at work. These policies protect our employees. They guide employees to behave in an appropriate way and provide a reference point for any employees who may feel harassed.

Although you overload yourself—and push the boundaries of your personal skills—you must never overstep NASS' formal boundaries. You push yourself to do better and achieve more, but you must do so within the company's ethical and formal structure. In other words, you demonstrate your will to advance in your career by working hard and adding value to your job functions, but you do not get ahead by trying to bypass or circumvent the company's policies, processes, and procedures.

We also need to discuss a different kind of boundary. To illustrate the importance of personal physical boundaries, I'd like to recount a true story. Once you read it, you will understand how setting boundaries protects our security officers. Here it is:

One day, a tenant arrived home at her condo complex carrying four heavy grocery bags. The security officer at the site opened the door for her. He asked her if he could help her with her packages. Grateful for a helping hand, the tenant handed him two bags and they took the elevator to her apartment. As soon as they reached her door, he put the bags down. The tenant turned to the security officer and asked whether he would mind putting the bags on her kitchen table. He had no problem with this request. After he had placed the bags on the counter, she thanked him and he left.

A week later, the tenant came home with more big bags of groceries. Again, the security officer offered to help. When they arrived at her condo, the tenant invited the security officer in for a cup of tea. He accepted the offer. They chatted about everyday things and after he finished his tea, he returned to his post.

Another week went by, and the tenant came home with a new batch of groceries. She was in a rush this time; as she had to get ready for a night out. When the security officer placed the grocery bags on her kitchen counter, he asked: "So, where's the tea?" The tenant, feeling violated, curtly thanked him and suggested that he leave.

What happened? By asking for the tea, the security officer overstepped the tenant's boundaries. However innocent his remark, it provoked the tenant to reinstate a boundary that she felt he had violated. A few days later, the security company received a call from condo management. The tenant had complained about the invasion of her space. She complained that she felt harassed. The security officer had to move from the site because he no longer felt comfortable there.

As security professionals, we must remain beyond reproach.

The security officer should have set his own boundaries. Although tea may have been appealing, **the officer could have protected himself** by saying: "I'd like to help you put your groceries in the kitchen, and tea sounds great, but I'm not permitted in your private space, unless it's an emergency."

Had the security officer called attention to a boundary related to his professional obligations, he would have remained beyond reproach. Whether or not his intentions were innocent, once the tenant felt violated, her complaint compromised the security officer's sense of comfort at his work place. So, both the formal boundaries we set at NASS and the personal boundaries that we encourage our security officers to set, protect our employees and give them strength.

Had Eric and I respected the boundaries of the marked trail on the climb up the mountain (designed for novice hikers), we never would have gotten into harm's way. There is safety in boundaries.

Ethical Living

By understanding the difference between our personal morals and the company's ethics we can make better decisions at work.

Your personal code of ethics is subjective. In other words, your morals are personal and you yourself choose, shape, and change them. The policies, processes, and procedures of a company and the client are not subjective. They are objective. In other words, they must be followed because they have been implemented for a reason. Unlike our own personal morals, we cannot choose to follow some of the company's ethics and ignore others.

The distinction between right and wrong behavior is often straightforward. The Bible states: "Thou shalt not steal." Sometimes, however, clear definitions between right and wrong become more difficult to see. There are often gray areas. At these moments, you must weigh the pros and the cons, and apply your own, subjective ethics to make a decision. Despite your personal feelings and inclinations, however, you must enforce and follow the company's ethical rules at all times.

Most commercial buildings, for instance, have a "no rollerblading" policy. Even capable rollerbladers are less stable on wheels than on their feet. In addition, their speed can frighten other patrons; the wheels can mark the floor. In other words, rollerbladers can be a significant liability for the building owner. A security officer might feel, however, that the risks of rollerblading are diminished during off-hours, when he or she is the only person in the building.

Rollerblading is unacceptable even during off-hours. **Regardless of your personal views, you must follow the rules of the site at all times.** Only then can we ensure consistency in our services. Our clients depend on us to be reliable. Policies exist for a reason. We implemented many of our policies years ago. The fact that these policies still exist—their persistence—proves that they work. By complying with them at all times, we have developed long, trusting relationships with our clients.

As a security officer, you represent the company you work for. While on duty, you take on the company's ethical code. In our profession, being ethical means following the rules of the client and the company as dictated in its policies, processes, and procedures.

Living Beyond Reproach

Imagine the following scenario: a security officer working at a high-security-level building escorts a guest into a secure space. To enter the space, the visitor must enter a personal identification number (PIN) into a touch pad. You can turn your back or tell the guest that you are not looking while they punch in their PIN. Even if you have access to the area, it is important to show the visitor that his or her privacy is protected.

Now let's consider another example. It may seem harmless for a security officer to help himself/herself to discarded items, such as leftover treats or drinks that will otherwise be thrown out. The security officer might see the treats as a perk of the job. But you have no right to take these items. The chances are that the client will notice and may cast your trustworthiness into question. If a computer goes missing the next day, fingers might be pointed in your direction. This might be hard to believe, but I have seen this logic at work. Clients who notice a security officer treating himself to one of their soft drinks might wonder whether he will treat himself to other items, things that the security officer is hired to protect. As security officers, we must be extremely careful about this. For instance, if a client offers you an occasional doughnut, you don't want to offend her by refusing. But her offer is not an open-ended invitation to help yourself to treats at every opportunity.

As security officers, we must act professionally enough to rule out any possibility of criticism. The nature of our job requires that the clients have complete trust in us: the client needs to know that we will not only protect their site from outsiders, but that we, on the inside, will respect the rules. By behaving with integrity, we will convince our clients that we are beyond reproach.

Chapter Six
Effective Communication and Team Work
The Virtual Private Network

"The achievements of an organization are the result of the combined effort of each individual."

Vince Lombardi

Expecting Excellence

Once we have had the pleasure of experiencing excellent customer service—whether at a hotel or in a taxicab—we come to expect excellent customer service everywhere. The way we form our expectations of customer service differs from the way we form our expectations of products. We do not expect the quality of one product to transfer to the next. In other words, we do not expect the special features in our car, such as air conditioning, to pop up in our TV – they are distinct products. With customer service, however, we do transfer our expectations from one situation to another.

Imagine: a security officer working at the entrance of a commercial complex greets you politely and with confidence, gives you clear directions, and then wishes you a good day. He has put you in a good mood. Why? Because he was **knowledgeable**— clearly an expert in this terrain (remember the mountain guy?) and **friendly**. So off you go to find the store he has pointed out to you. You need to buy a new toaster. You find the toaster you want, and you go to pay for it. The cashier at the counter doesn't make eye contact, grunts a hello, and handles your purchase carelessly, tossing it into a plastic bag. You're annoyed by his attitude. Because the security officer gave you excellent customer service, you don't accept the cashier's rudeness and indifference.

We're all human and we all have bad days. But the security officer's professionalism makes you more inclined to file a complaint about the cashier to the store's manager. Let's say that you actually do speak with the store's manager. Let's say that you want to be fair. So you might tell the manager that if the cashier is usually personable, then you're willing to overlook this lapse, if the manager promises to have a quiet chat with him later on. But if the cashier's rudeness is habitual, you may want to write a strong letter of complaint.

This example reveals how our expectations of customer service translate from one situation to another. When we experience excellent customer service, we raise our standards and we grow to expect excellent customer service everywhere.

Imagine how pleasant life would be if everyone made an effort to serve their customers with a smile and a personable disposition!

Consistency

You've been to McDonalds, right? We've all had a Big Mac and all Big Macs taste the same. Despite the fact that in Australia the wrappers around Big Macs have a kangaroo on them, whereas in Canada the Big Macs wrappers have a maple leaf on them, a Big Mac is a Big Mac is a Big Mac, no matter where you are. We expect a certain quality—taste, texture, thickness—in a McDonalds burger. And McDonalds consistently meets our standards. **One way we ensure quality is by consistently meeting customer expectations.**

How does McDonalds manage to make the same burger every time? I'll tell you how: they have standardized their processes and equipment to ensure absolute consistency in their product.

At NASS, we wanted to produce a similar consistency in our customer service. Although we take many measures to hire and train motivated employees, the growth and demographics of the industry are such that, once in a while, we hire an employee who does not quite reach the high level we demand. We value each and every employee and each and every client. That is why we looked into the possibility of developing a process-system that all employees could access to become adept at providing **consistently high levels of service.**

If, for instance, we train a team of 10 security officers and nine of the 10 are top notch, but one remains weak, the representative quality of the entire group drops. In other words, **we're only as strong as our weakest link.** If that person serves a customer who then gives negative feedback, our revenue for the entire group of 10 may be lowered because of the poor work of the one. In other words, the nine top-notch employees are paid less because one employee provides a lower quality of service.

Since the quality of that one team member's work can lower the salary of the other nine, we wanted to help that team member to raise his or her performance. We asked ourselves how we could help improve his or her standard of service, so that it could be raised as close as possible to the standards of the others – consistently. **In short, how could we standardize our customer service?**

In the early nineties, we began to brainstorm methods that would help us ensure consistency in delivery of service. There must be a way, we thought, to continually and reliably provide top-notch, motivated employees.

Nearly a decade ago we began to create a system that functions in such a way that our employees, once plugged in, could deliver excellent customer service and feel motivated to do so all the time. We call it the **Virtual Private Network, or VPN.**

This initiative has cost NASS millions of dollars, but it has proven to be an excellent investment. It has transformed our company. Because of our commitment to continuous improvement, NASS created the VPN to motivate our staff and to make them feel connected to the company and to each other.

Here's How It Works:

Since our security officers often have to work in isolation, being able to interact with other employees at NASS through the VPN develops their sense of belonging. Our company is quite large, and our security officers often work in distant cities or regions, far apart from one another. Every employee plays a very valuable role in our company and each one has an important function to perform. If they didn't, our clients would not hire us. Often, however, security officers do not see how valuable they are. Our services are provided 24 hours a day, 365 days a year (since many of our customers require continuous service in different geographic locations): how can we give our security officers leadership? How can we train them? How can we give them adequate supervision? How can we support them?

Observing and reporting are two key components of a security officer's work. In the past, when we used to take over sites, I would examine the desk that had been used by the previous security company's guard. In his desk drawer I would usually find a pile of reports, spanning the period from the beginning of his employment to his termination. The first report would be lengthy and detailed, showing attentive observation and care. A report written a month later would be half the length of the first and quite vague. The building manager might have read the report but given no feedback to the employee. This second month report was clearly less complete than the first. The final report, written just before the security officer's termination, often had no more than a few lines on it and it was of little value.

The deterioration of the reports was not entirely the fault of the security officer. After all, why would he want to write thorough, detailed reports when no one would read them? And even if they were read, the form of the report did not facilitate feedback.

Let's say that a light in the hallway of a building burns out. The security officer reports it because he knows that the veil of darkness increases the feeling of anonymity that can incite criminal behavior. So he reports it. The following night, he finds that the light is still burnt out. He writes a second report. By the third day, if the light has still not been changed, more often than not, the security officer will assume that no one has read his report. This may not be the case, but since no one had given him feedback as to why his report has not been acted upon, this is what he concludes.

It's possible that the building manager *did* read the officer's report, but since the lighting contractor isn't due to come to the building for a few weeks, the manager decided not to act on it. It's also possible that the manager read the report but was so busy that he put the task on his "to-do" list and forgot to notify the security officer. In both scenarios, the security officer is left out of the loop.

Why? Well, the security officer works the night-shift and the building manager usually works during the day. Moreover, the security officer works for the security company and the building manager works for the owner of the complex.

This situation exemplifies a common breakdown in communication. This breakdown results in the demoralization of the security officer and the deterioration of his or her performance. In the end, his or her poor performance leads to termination.

We set up the VPN in such a way that every single report a security officer writes is read by someone on the leadership team (who is usually the security officer's direct supervisor). The security officer receives regular feedback when and where needed. Interacting with supervisors over the VPN ensures security officers feel that their work is acknowledged and has meaning. What's more, the feedback provided to security officers on their reports has improved our staff's learning curve, because the supervisor (or mentor) can give an officer useful tips on improving his reports. By providing constructive feedback, the VPN helps to motivate and to educate our personnel while keeping them in the loop.

Through the VPN, security officers know when they have done a good job because the supervisor gives them timely feedback online. Similarly, the VPN enables the supervisor to let the officer know when a report needs to be expanded or when certain points need more investigation.

In addition, we make all reports available to our clients (through the VPN). Our customers can then provide their own feedback to the supervisor or directly to the employee, reinforcing our commitment to "partnership." The VPN also allows us to evaluate the performance of our security officers because we can pull their files from the database. We have partitioned files for every security officer.

To avoid a biased evaluation by one person of any of our employees, NASS' internal clients — the site supervisors, the control centre, the payroll department, etc.— can also collectively participate in the evaluation of a security officer's performance. In this way we provide the officer and ourselves with a full understanding of his or her strengths and weaknesses. We encourage both internal and external clients to give our security officers positive reinforcement as well as constructive criticism.

Human Resources personnel can give each security officer an electronic notice of his evaluation. He can electronically respond to the comments of his internal and external clients. He can write down his own thoughts about the feedback compiled in his secure file. All of us—even the coaches and supervisors—have room to grow in our jobs and in our lives. We are committed to the continuous development of each team member and of the corporation as a whole.

Let's review: why did we build the VPN? **To connect our staff, to emphasize their significance in the company, and to make us all smarter.** You see, we gave the VPN the name SmartNet. The word "SMART" in the name stands for "Standardized Management and Report Trending." We use the VPN to generate trend reports. These are compiled monthly, quarterly, or semi-annually according to the needs of each client. For instance, a trend report enables us to note that at 6 p.m. every Tuesday a security officer reports seeing an insecure door at his site. The trend report makes us aware that someone is propping open that door every Tuesday at the same time and is compromising the building's integrity. The analysis also enables us to make the appropriate hardware changes, or take other preventative and corrective steps at our sites. Trend reports enable us to find the root cause of problems.

During the initial development of the VPN, we conceptualized three virtual platforms. The first one we incorporated into the system was directed toward our front-line employees. We called this platform TeamNet because we wanted to emphasize that each employee is a team member. We hoped that if we could show our front-line staff the value of their work, we could reinforce their morale, their diligence and their professionalism.

Within the TeamNet platform, we compiled useful information for our team members: knowledge we have accumulated over the years. TeamNet also features shift and incident reports and feedback **templates** that guide security officers through the process of answering questions. The report templates help security officers provide more thorough reports with more relevant information.

In addition, we include **training material** within the platform, as well as other **supportive information**. For example, team members can use the tools on the platform to request a uniform component, a request we can act upon the following day.

Then there is **scheduling**. We find that this is crucial to employee satisfaction. We all want to know our schedules in advance and we have found that both officers and supervisors tend to want consistency in their schedules. In response to this desire, we show the employees' schedules on TeamNet. What's more, we also have secure (encrypted) partitioned portals that enable our clients to view their site-specific schedules because they understandably need and want to see consistency in their scheduling too. Also, posting schedules on SmartNet enables our managers to see where there may be scheduling conflicts that they need to work through. We post the schedules according to the needs of the viewers: our front-line personnel need to know their individual schedules, our clients require their site-specific schedules, and our leaders, supervisors and managers need to view all the work schedules within their portfolio.

To increase our staff's motivation, TeamNet also includes **payroll and benefit information** and **internal job postings**. This shows staff that promotions are available and within their reach, provided that they overload themselves and express their needs and interests in regards to advancement. *The Sentinel*, our online newsletter, includes recent employee awards, which give employees a sense of acknowledgement and motivation. The *Sentinel* also enhances a sense of community and corporate culture.

SmartNet also has an automated feedback **call-monitor system** to ensure that security officers are on duty at their clients' sites. The system functions in real time, and is monitored 24 hours a day. Furthermore, the fact that employees can punch in (sign-in) online increases payroll efficiency and accuracy.

To further support our field security officers, NASS engages **control centre** operators who oversee all operations. The online information that they deal with is in real time. The control centre is synonymous with the nerve centre of NASS.

Policies, processes, and procedures are always available online for quick reference by security personnel. Workshops are available online to promote continuous development and to foster ongoing career interests. The employee suggestion box is also available online – and all suggestions submitted receive feedback.

To summarize, TeamNet creates a two-way flow of information between front-line staff and the head office. New employees can familiarize themselves with NASS' corporate culture, benefits and opportunities, in an efficient, organized, and **user-friendly** way.

Let's go on to review other aspects of the VPN, so that you can gain a greater understanding of the company in which you play a crucial role.

My leadership team has demonstrated such devotion to the company over the years that at times I worried that they might overload themselves to the point of experiencing negative stress. I wanted to construct a platform that would support them in their work.

The second platform – CoachesNet - has many online tools that increase the company's efficiency, which in turn enables our leaders to direct their energy toward other crucial matters. We call our supervisors "coaches" because they mentor and educate our front-line staff. CoachesNet supports the efforts of our coaches by also providing them with a reliable resource where they can learn more about management. It is the second platform of SmartNet. The coaches assist our front-line staff in their endeavours to become providers of excellent security and customer service. The coaches explain, educate, supervise, and discipline, if necessary. Accordingly, CoachesNet consists of useful information about leadership and mentoring.

We use the name PartnersNet to refer to the last platform we included in our initial vision of the VPN. We geared this platform toward our clients, whom we see as partners because of the collaborative nature of our work. Our objective has always been to serve our clients by ensuring that we fully understand their needs. Good communication is key to our relationship with our customers. Indeed, it is key to our relationship with everyone involved in the company, including coaches and team members.

Over the years, we noticed that clients expressed an interest in items such as site work instructions, incident reports, work schedules, etc., were of interest to most of our clients. PartnersNet addresses these elements. As mentioned, our clients—property and facility managers, for instance—benefit from having continuous access to the information that pertains to their buildings. Just as our team members understand the value of their work because SmartNet keeps them in the loop with regards to matters of relevance to them, so we show our partners how much we value them by constructing a site devoted to enhancing client satisfaction.

TeamNet, CoachesNet, and PartnersNet are partitioned and encrypted. Team members, coaches, and partners have access to the parts of the system that pertain to them. Why, for instance, would we trouble a project manager by forcing him to scroll down the schedules of other sites to reach his own building's schedule? We offer him access to his site-specific schedule, the incidents at his sites, and his site-work instructions. Similarly, we don't want to distract a team member by showing him the incidents at a site where he does not work. By using partitions within SmartNet, we provide each person with the information of relevance to him or her.

About a year after the completion of the first full VPN, my leadership team, my IT team and I sat down at my home to draw up our five-year IT plan. We discussed our vision for the years ahead. Although we were thrilled about the development of SmartNet, it occurred to us that evening that we could construct a fourth VPN platform. Since many of our client's clients – the tenants of complexes, for instance – often approached us with questions, we decided to create the TenantNet. We would devote this platform to answering the pertinent questions asked by our partners' clients.

Today, this platform reinforces our goal of providing excellent customer service and security. We want our clients' tenants to be familiar with the security protocols provided for their safety. Their awareness gives them a greater sense of safety and security in their workspace. TenantNet gives our clients' clients access to such things as concierge services, access control registers, and specific fire-plans. In short, TenantNet is fully customizable and can easily include the following categories: News and Events, Policies and Procedures, Security Services, Building Services Requests, Car-Pooling and Contact Information.

Although this platform was not included in our initial vision of the VPN, we developed it in accordance with our commitment to continuous improvement.

SmartNet has led to unparalleled operational efficiencies and heightened quality delivery utilities. This project was a huge undertaking. And like most innovations, it was met with some resistance. It took time for people to adapt to writing reports online after they had been hand-written for decades. Today, one of the many advantages of SmartNet is that the on-line reporting system ensures that all reports are legible. The system has been years in the making and will continue to evolve.

Some of our partners also initially expressed concerns about the VPN. We listened to their concerns and built features into the system to reassure them. For instance, our security officers (team members) cannot surf the web during their shifts. They only have access to authorized sites that support the work they do for the clients. Examples of authorized sites may include CNN and The Weather Network since team members need to stay up to date on current events. Other examples of authorized sites might include the particular home-page of the client. If, for instance, a team member provides security and customer service for a pharmaceutical company, he will have access to the company's homepage. In this way, he can familiarize himself with his client. Another security officer, working at an office complex, will have access to the property manager's homepage. In other words, our personnel are able to focus on their responsibilities because the computers on site only give them access to the appropriate portals. In this way, we maximize efficiency and ensure that the VPN reinforces the security officer's capacity to provide excellent customer service and security.

SmartNet occupies a central, transforming position in our company. It is crucial that I emphasize, however, that SmartNet is not the work we do. **We are in the customer service security business. We help people. That's our work. We save lives and help people to enrich their lives.** The VPN simply **facilitates** our objectives.

Staying Current

A key part of your job involves referring to site orders, post orders, and memos. You refer to these habitually to make sure that you are on top of all your necessary tasks. **Site orders** are written duties and procedures that a security officer must follow at a site. These include such things as access control, emergency protocols, and alarm response procedures. **Post orders** are specific written instructions for a particular post, including timelines for the accomplishment of tasks. These explain the responsibilities that a security officer must fulfill while working at a certain station. **Memos** notify an officer of a temporary change to a site or post order. The detailed daily memos mention the duration of the change and the security officer's new responsibility. You must read the memos (*pass-ons*), delivered over the SmartNet system, before every shift.

Just as NASS managers' lists are in a constant state of change, the security officer's lists are habitually updated. The instructions change as your environment changes. People come and go, special events and renovations occur at sites, tenants move, and new technologies arrive. These changes are reflected in operational changes and in changes to your daily routines. In other words, site orders, post-orders, and memos *(pass-ons)* reflect the changes that occur at your site. So, you must review these on a regular basis. (Again, in the case of memos, you review them before each shift.)

NASS also uses checklists and forms for incident reports. **Checklists** prompt you; they remind you what to look for, what to ask for, etc. They are not a substitute for thinking. They are meant as reference materials, a guide to ensure that things don't fall through the cracks. They are like "to-do" lists; you constantly refer to the checklists for reassurance that the necessary tasks have been completed, the proper questions have been asked, and the crucial observations have been recorded.

To further ensure that things aren't missed, one day soon, our staff will access these checklists through portable Palm Pilots or PDAs. Currently, most security officers patrol with notebook and pen in hand...

...They then return to the security console and type the information into an online document. However, with the advancement of electronic forms, security officers will soon be directing the information to the control centre within seconds of their observation. These electronic checklists ensure that you complete each task, report its completion, and provide feedback when necessary. The information the security officer provides is uploaded in NASS' VPN, where the control centre can access and act on it immediately. By prompting security officers to capture the most thorough information at the point of collection, it ensures that NASS' employees are less likely to miss items.

Currently, more than 90% of NASS' full and part-time staff is fully connected to the VPN. Research demonstrates that our security officers are learning faster with the implementation of this system. The company and its customers benefit from robust, concise reporting, follow-up, and closure to all tasks.

Chapter Seven
Effective Communication
Say What You Mean and Mean What You Say

"Communication is like a dance. One person takes a step forward, the other takes a step back. Even one misstep can land both on the floor in a tangle of confusion. That's the perfect moment to rise to your feet and get clear about the next move—to gently say to the other dancer, 'What do you really want here?'"

Oprah Winfrey

"Those who shape our destiny, the giants who teach us and inspire us, are those who use words with clarity, grandeur, and passion."

Peggy Anderson, writer

In our profession, we interact with people regularly. However, we sometimes experience difficulties in getting our message across or understanding exactly what someone is trying to say. In this chapter, we will examine why communication problems arise and how we can communicate more effectively.

CARE is a useful acronym for remembering some elements of effective communication.

- **C**areful
- **A**nnunciation with
- **R**e-transmission and
- **E**xplanation

Obviously, it's impossible to communicate by direct mind-to-mind contact. Information from the sender is always filtered through the receiver's interpretive Personality Screen. This is a form of selective hearing shaped by a person's past experiences, culture, and beliefs. Personality screens filter the intended message because of each receiver's unique perceptions; the source's message is rarely understood as intended, at least initially.

Because of these screens, some information comes in, other information stays out. In the end, the receiver absorbs information that has been cut up, mixed up and re-shaped. In short, the receiver can interpret a message in a way that differs from the speaker's original intention.

The personality screen is "on" at all times. It filters every remark, be it a joke, a comment, a compliment or a criticism.

Here's how it works: Person A sends a message. The information passes through the personality screen of Person B. By the time Person B gets the information, it has been changed. The words remain the same but the meaning is different. What Person B does with the information is then based on his or her interpretation of the message. This phenomenon of distortion or misinterpretation makes communication difficult at times.

Let's take the simple question "How are you?" One person might interpret this as a genuine inquiry into one's feelings. Another might hear it as routine, meaningless small talk and answer "Fine" without thinking about it further. Yet another person might perceive the question as intrusive and nosy. No matter how seemingly simple the question, it could be interpreted in a multitude of ways depending on each receiver's unique personality screen.

Personality screens are built in. They're a part of who we are, how we perceive the world, hear and communicate. All of us have come from different starting places and have experienced different personality-shaping events along the way. When you understand how personality screens can complicate communication, you begin to realize that you must be conscious of how you communicate. You begin to understand why you might have to explain yourself at times. For instance, if a receiver interprets the question, "How are you?" as an intrusive and rude one, the person who asked the question may have to explain that he/she meant it as a harmless pleasantry and might have to explain that they didn't mean to pry.

We will all have moments when we are misunderstood. By acknowledging that everyone, including us, has a personality screen, we can better understand why we are, at times, misunderstood. By understanding personality screens, we can become more effective communicators.

Security Officers and the Personality Screen

As a security officer, taking personality screens into consideration will help you to write reports, follow working instructions more precisely, and better interact with your peers, clients and managers. Whether you are communicating verbally or in writing, you must always be as clear as possible and minimize the room for interpretation.

When you find yourself on the receiving end of a message, take the time to listen carefully and then ask for clarification. Do this two, three, four, or as many times as necessary, to ensure that you understand exactly what the person is saying.

Troubled interaction comes from problematic communication. You can strive to avoid this. There is nothing wrong with repeating and clarifying what you have to say in order to achieve crystal clear communication.

Clarity

When you write reports, you must choose your words carefully. You must try to be as objective as possible. In other words, you must give a detailed account of the facts without being swayed by emotion. You must refrain from labeling people. If a person is rude to you, for instance, don't use a swear word to describe what he did. If you recount the incident in detail, without emotion, the supervisor reading the report will still be able to see that the person was rude. Try not to let your feelings direct or control what you write. Write your report, then re-read it to make sure it still says what you want it to, prior to submitting it.

You must read carefully. In written documents, instructions, and site orders, words have been chosen intentionally to convey a particular message. Throughout this book, for example, important ideas are repeated several times to make sure the message is understood the way it is intended. Different readers will have different personality screens and may interpret the key messages of each chapter differently. However, by repeating and emphasizing the main points, I hope to reduce the effects of personality screens.

Give clear directions. As security officers, you help people find their way by using three methods of communication: verbal instructions, written instructions, and gestures. Some buildings also have signage to which people can refer.

Some people navigate by referring to north, south, east, and west. (Be careful using "right" and "left" because these vary according to the angle from which a person approaches an area.) Others prefer to navigate by using landmarks. If asked, for example, how to find a museum, one security officer might say, "Go four blocks south, turn west, and it's four blocks ahead on the north side of the street." Another security officer might say: "Head four blocks in the direction of the white tower, turn left towards the Texaco station, and it's four blocks ahead on the same side of the street as the art gallery." Or the security officer could draw a map. All of these ways of giving directions are acceptable, since they all explain how to reach the museum. Depending on how a person's mind works, however, he or she will respond better to one of these methods than to the others. If the directions a security officer gives are initially misunderstood, the officer must remember to repeat them in a different way.

Eye Contact and Facial Expressions

The most successful communication occurs in real time and face-to-face. The Transmitter's eye contact, facial expressions, and body language help the receiver to interpret the information.

E-mail and text-messages may include details, but they do not include gestures and vocal tones that complement and clarify communication.

Two-way radios (the kind where you have to push a button to talk, and release it to listen), allow only one person to talk at a time. Misunderstandings often occur because of poor transmission and background noise—physical barriers to communication.

Whenever possible, it's best to communicate face-to-face because this form of communication is supported by factors that can help to clarify your message. If this isn't possible, take the time to communicate clearly, using details and a strongly projected voice.

Then ask the receiver to paraphrase—repeat in their own words—what you have said. This way, you can confirm that your message has been received the way you intended.

Transmitting

To improve the transmission (sending) of your messages:
- Think in advance about the point you're trying to make.
- Be sensitive and aware of varying personality screens.
- Express the point in a thoughtful, thorough manner.
- Ask for feedback to ensure that the message is understood.

Receiving

To improve your reception of messages:
- Listen carefully to the question or message.
- Make sure you understand each word when reading a work instruction, site orders, policies, processes or procedures. If you don't understand, ask someone. There's never anything wrong with asking. For instance, you could say: "I just wanted to make sure that 'efficiency' meant in the most time-saving, effective manner possible." Or you could simply ask someone to "clarify the meaning of the word 'efficient'." By asking, you show your curiosity and attentiveness.
- Watch the speaker's body language, facial expressions, and gestures.
- Concentrate on the speaker. Tune out other distractions and noises.

Re-Transmitting the Message

After you've sent the message, send it again. Repeat the information in the message to ensure that it was understood. People use different parts of their brain. If the Transmitter sends the message in multiple, varied ways, the receiver is likely to be able to receive it in at least one way.

Let's look at an example. If someone ignores the "No Trespassing" signs, and enters a blocked corridor, a security officer must send a clear verbal message that the area is off limits. "Please

don't use the north corridor. Please use the south corridor, instead."
By saying this, the message is given (…don't use the north
corridor). And the message is also repeated by offering an
alternative (….please use the south corridor…). And it's said in a
polite way (…please…).

Let's look at another example. A co-worker who asks for
the time over a two-way radio might find it difficult to hear the
answer. Or perhaps English is not his first language. If, after you've
repeated the simplest answer a few times—"it's 9:40 am"—the co-
worker still can't understand, try saying it a different way. "In 20
minutes it will be 10 o'clock." By using your creativity and sending
the message in a different way, you facilitate understanding. The
message remains the same.

Feedback

In the children's game, "Broken Telephone," each player
has only one chance to whisper a specific message in the ear of the
player next to them. Without fail, by the time this message gets
around the circle, it has drastically changed. The new interpretation
of the message isn't intentional; it simply reflects how different
players misheard and misinterpreted the words passed on to them. If
the players had had the opportunity to hear the message one more
time, the chances that they would hear the correct message would
greatly increase. If the players had had limitless opportunities to
hear and then repeat the message aloud, the final player would have
understood the message loud and clear.

In the real world, misconstrued messages are often passed
along. Unlike the players in the game of Broken Telephone,
however, we have ample opportunities as well an obligation to
clarify the messages we send. We do so through **feedback**.

Feedback is a tool that assists us to overcome
misinterpretations. By asking receivers to confirm their
interpretation of a message (this is the feedback) you have the
opportunity to clarify your message if required. Back and forth, the
sender and receiver discuss what was meant by the message until it
becomes completely clear.

Imagine the following scenario: officer Ted transmits a message to customer Bill, who hears the message through his individual personality screen (filter). Customer Bill misinterprets the message as an offensive remark. Customer Bill responds (gives feedback) with angry words and gestures. However, realizing that he may have misunderstood the message, customer Bill asks, "Is that what you meant to say?" Officer Ted then clarifies his message, revealing that it wasn't intended to be offensive. Both Bill and Ted bounce comments back and forth until the intention of the original message becomes clear. Through feedback, officer Ted and customer Bill manage to avoid a potential conflict. If the communication had ended after the first transmission, both parties might have responded irrationally, and started an argument.

Don't always assume you're clearly understood. Getting feedback is the key to confirming your message was "received and understood."

Sometimes feedback must be solicited—that is, you have to ask for it. To illustrate, customer Cathy asks security officer Dan: "Where can I find the washrooms?" Security officer Dan gives her the directions and then asks: "Are my directions clear?" Customer Cathy might then repeat back what she thought she heard, which may make it necessary for security officer Dan to clarify. He may have to say: "Actually, you have to go up the escalator, not down." Again, feedback was the key. It's just that this time it was asked for rather than volunteered.

Miscommunication in the Security Profession

About 99 percent of the people who interact with security officers want to be cooperative. They want people boarding an aircraft to be thoroughly inspected, they want clear directions at a rock concert, they want thorough access control systems at the workplace, etc.

Miscommunication, however, often makes people *seem* uncooperative.

Miscommunication can also make you feel ineffective. Miscommunication occurs when the speaker fails to produce the intended response and when the listener does not comprehend the speaker's message. Through feedback and clarification, you can overcome instances of miscommunication.

When security officers have to enforce rules in a building, people who don't understand the message can appear to be breaking the rules. In every situation, you, as security officers, must approach our clients, managers, and customers with a customer service mindset. In other words, you must approach instances of miscommunication with a friendly disposition and a willingness to work through the communication problem by using feedback.

Avoid jumping to conclusions. As people who deliver customer service, we try to clarify, explain, and repeat information in different ways. If you are polite and helpful, you are more likely to succeed in helping others understand.

As security officers, you always reserve the option to "pump up the volume" to reach that small percentage of people who aren't cooperative. These people might well understand the intention of the message; they just don't agree with it. You may have to communicate with them in a more assertive way.

Communication is a skill that you must continue to develop throughout your life. You can never predict how a receiver will filter your message, and you must clarify your messages through repetition and variation. When you are the one receiving a message, remember to paraphrase to ensure that you have clearly understood the message. Remember, each of us is unique and we all have unique personality screens.

Chapter Eight
What You Learn at Work, You Learn for Life.

My experiences on the mountain enriched my professional life, as you can see. Similarly, the lessons we draw from the workplace can improve the quality of our lives outside of work:

Recently, it became clear to one of NASS' supervisors that a NASS employee had a communication problem. Every time the employee felt dissatisfied, he vocalized it—aggressively, and with profanity. Although the employee was performing his job very well, his negative attitude made those who worked with him miserable. His supervisor focused on the problem and suggested ways for the employee to moderate his tone of voice, cut out the swear words, and express his concerns to management in a structured, formal way.

The employee's supervisor worked with the individual and encouraged him to deal with his frustrations in a controlled way. The employee wasn't aware of the extent to which he swore until he started to work with this supervisor.

The employee's wife recalled how her husband used to come home from work feeling stressed out and how he would vent his frustrations loudly in front of their children. Usually, an argument between the couple would ensue: she would ask him to stop swearing, he would continue to yell, and the kids would start crying. Soon neither partner could remember how the fight began as the topic switched from money, to chores, to family, and to their personal relationship.

However, since the catalytic talk with the supervisor, the wife acknowledged that things had started to change. Her husband rarely came home in a foul mood anymore, and if he did, the couple discussed their feelings calmly. She couldn't explain it, but somehow her husband seemed happier at work now, and that happiness translated into a happier home life as well.

Our work is a big part of our lives; the skills that we learn and exercise at work will have a positive spillover effect at home.

In the workplace, the supervisor could easily diagnose and treat the communication problem. The employee and his wife couldn't see the real problem because their emotions were a barrier to communication. When stressed, it is very difficult to pinpoint the underlying cause of our frustrations.

The supervisor assumed the role of a mentor. Emotionally detached from the situation, the supervisor helped the employee with constructive criticism. The employee knew that if he didn't make an effort to improve his behaviour, he might lose his job. In contrast, the consequences for bad behaviour at home seemed minimal. His wife, he assumed, would not "fire" him.

Let's look at a problem in our industry—the bad habit of being late. If you're late for work, the chances are that you're late for personal engagements as well. Habitual lateness at work can get you fired. In your personal life, however, the consequences of being late may seem minimal. But tardiness is inconsiderate and it certainly angers friends and family.

Work is a microcosm of life. That is why NASS demands that our security officers work on two aspects of their development: the work of the organization and their work as an individual.

The Work of the Organization

Depending on their position, NASS security officers and supervisors and executives have specific duties to fulfill: report writing, patrols, access control, customer service, preventative and corrective tasks, etc. Employees, however, also have the responsibility to work on their position. This means designing ways to become more effective at their jobs. **NASS' corporate culture encourages innovations that improve the quality of service delivery.**

In the security industry, quality can only be achieved by having highly trained and highly motivated personnel fulfilling the clients' expectations. Employees at every level of the organization must be fully engaged in their respective duties. By adding value to their individual jobs, employees enhance the work of the organization. Improving one's work as an individual improves the overall work of the organization.

The Work of the Individual

At NASS, we believe that improvements in a person's life will carry over into their work and vice versa. We want our employees to be well rounded and happy. In fact, NASS demands that our employees reach their highest potential by developing the four skills: **concentration, organization, innovation,** and **communication.**

Concentration means focusing and sustaining your attention. **Organization** means creating order. **Innovative ideas** can lead to positive actions. And **communication** helps you effectively practice necessary procedures.

At NASS, each employee starts as an apprentice, and gets training in these four areas. As employees develop, they become Client Relation Specialists (CRS) and Accredited Protection Professionals (APP). With time, APP become coaches for new APP. Coaches focus on the development of employees as well as their own continuing development. The honing of these four skills— concentration, organization, innovation, and communication—is life-long. Coaches keep learning, too.

Work is a training ground for the outside world. As we saw in the earlier example, the employee's efforts to improve his communication skills at work had a positive impact on both the quality of his work experience and the quality of his home life. **Consider employment as a life-long workshop on life-skills.**

The Accredited Protection Professional (APP) Pledge

The APP is one of NASS' registered trademarks. Our security officers earn this accreditation through NASS' proprietary training programs. All NASS employees adhere to the APP pledge. It states:

"I will practice the core values of North American Security Services which include a self- responsibility to make my work challenging

and enjoyable; to attend work with a positive attitude regardless of outside factors; and to assist all of my teammates to the best of my abilities. I understand that I am expected not to do the bare minimum but to find every opportunity to add value to my work, which will enrich me, my employer, and our clients."

In some companies, it might seem unusual for employees to fulfill more than the expected requirements of their positions. At NASS, it's customary. Our corporate culture nurtures security officers and managers who instinctively strive to go above and beyond the call of duty.

Let's step outside our industry for a moment and consider the following, inspiring example. Consider how this individual uses his skills to be of service to others. Also consider how the skills he learned at work carry over to other aspects of his life.

A few years ago, I heard about an elite personal trainer who used highly effective words of encouragement while "whipping" his clients into shape. When I heard about André Maillé, I did not believe that a trainer could help me improve my workout through his language and gestures. In the past, the trainers I worked with simply supervised a rotational workout routine and gave advice on the proper ways to do things. This got the job done. Well, actually, on second thought, it didn't. I never stuck with the routine.

Then I met André. He is a winner of the Mr. World Body Building Competition. When I heard about him, he was working at the local gym. When I called to book an appointment, he insisted on coming out of his way and meeting me at my office. He arrived early, and he spent the entire hour asking me questions. He wanted to know about my work schedule, my typical workday, my past fitness experiences, my fitness goals. While we talked, his eyes never left mine. I felt like the centre of his universe. I've worked with André many times since that day, and each time he has given me 100 percent of his attention.

André motivates and monitors; he doesn't give orders. He moves quickly across the gym to get his client's weights. He presets machines, so that the entire hour is spent on working out...

...He understands that we all have low-energy days, but he motivates his clients even more on those days. At the end of a session, he congratulates the client on a job well done He shakes the client's hand and reminds them of the time and day of the next training session. He thanks his clients for choosing him as their trainer. I, in turn, as one of his clients, thank André for choosing me as someone to believe in.

Every Sunday evening, André sits down and plans each client's workout schedule for the up-coming week. André knows that I thrive on challenge and change, so he modifies my routine every week, keeping in mind my target areas. If he foresees a scheduling conflict, he reworks his calendar to suit mine.

André's secret of success is simple: his job as a personal trainer allows him to provide a service to others, a service that makes them feel better about themselves.

It is André's commitment and continuing drive to find ways to add value to his clients' workouts that have set him apart from other trainers. It is those qualities that also helped him earn the Mr. World Body Building title.

In a sense, André has signed the APP Pledge. He has made it his life mission to rise above and beyond the bare minimum requirements that a trainer must fulfill, and to provide a superior service to his clients. He sees helping clients to achieve their goals as a personal challenge. He sees each training session as an opportunity to enjoy himself with his client. He has a positive attitude and he brings a desire to help his clients to each meeting, thereby enriching the lives of those that he assists, as well as his own.

Chapter Nine
A New Perspective on NASS' Core Values

"I'm a great believer in luck, and I find that the harder I work the more I have of it."

Thomas Jefferson

NASS has nineteen core values; many of them are interrelated. This chapter will review how these values are intertwined in our corporate culture and our daily behaviour.

NASS' Core Values

Accountability: To be responsible for someone or something. To see every task through to its completion.

Every action we initiate has an effect. Everything we do has consequences. Think about the words "accountable" and "accountability:" they obviously relate to the notion of counting on someone and others counting on us. Dependability—*being dependable*—is strongly related to accountability—being accountable.

Often we hear the excuse: "Sorry I'm late. Traffic was bad." But when you are accountable, you anticipate different volumes of traffic throughout the day, and you make sure to avoid heavy traffic and arrive at work on time. Remember the IGA example? In our company, you show your co-workers and internal and external customers that they can count on you by arriving at work at least 15 minutes early. Since you are accountable for your performance at work, you come to work well rested and prepared for your shifts.

We all have days when we are not at our best. You are always, however, accountable for the reports you write, which should be based on accurate and detailed observations. If, on one of those less than great days, you decide to skip a patrol, thinking that you can bypass the checks and balances, and an incident occurs, you will be held accountable. You will be held responsible for your poor judgment in deciding to skip the patrol. You will be held accountable for jeopardizing the integrity of the building's security.

I know that you're beginning to get a clear picture of accountability. Before moving on to the next core value, however, let's briefly discuss another extremely important idea that is closely connected to accountability: *judgment.* Before yelling at someone, for instance, you must think about the possible consequences of this action. By performing action "a"—in this case, yelling—will I generate "b"—in this case, embarrassment—or "c"— a lack of cooperation? Do I want either b or c? If the answer is no, then I should not perform "a." In other words, I shouldn't yell. If I do yell I will be accountable for my action. If I don't yell, I will also be accountable for that decision. Perhaps, after all, it *was* appropriate to shout to capture someone's attention (consequence d).

We are accountable for every action we take. When providing access control to a complex, you use your judgment to decide whom to allow into the building. If you do not scrutinize all visitors, and one of them engages in a confrontation with an employee, you will be accountable for your decision to allow the perpetrator into the complex. For every decision you make, you have to ask yourself: "What is the basis for my decision?"

We are ultimately accountable for our whole selves. The good habits we develop today will bring better actions and better results in our lives. Accountability means not pointing fingers. You are your own person—and you are accountable for everything you do.

> **"Cop" is an acronym. It stands for Constable on Patrol. We are Cops too; we are Citizens on Patrol.**

Attentiveness: To be alert and aware of every aspect of our environment. To notice everything.

You can ensure that you are attentive to details by coming to work warmed up and ready to engage in your tasks. Being attentive involves scrutinizing people, rather than just casually glancing at them. Being attentive also involves personalizing your interaction with your customers. Addressing clients by their last names shows your attention to detail. Writing your reports with precision also demonstrates your attention to detail. *Being attentive means being conscious and aware.* By being attentive to your environment you're more likely to pick up changes and potential security and safety hazards. We can't afford to be casual.

Caring Attitude: To behave in a kind, considerate and attentive manner.

Because you care about your working environment, you ask the tenants of the building how they are doing. You approach your environment as if you were a gardener. You are a guard standing over your individual garden, picking out weeds. You'll notice that since you care about our environment, you pay a lot of attention to details. Since you care, you take *ownership of your tasks*.

Continuous Improvement: We need to continually refine our skills. We build on what we already know. We engage in something at a deeper level.

A great example of continuous improvement involves communication: we must work on continuously developing the way we communicate with each other. If a teammate on a walkie-talkie asks you where you are, you shouldn't answer "I'm at the north side of the building." To be an effective communicator, you have to add details to the directions, such as "I'm at the north side of the building, in front of a red brick tower." By continuously improving your communication skills—by adding accurate details to your sentences, and by speaking clearly—you will be able to communicate effectively in emergencies. At these times, tension heightens and you need to communicate in an extra-clear, extra-crisp way. (See Chapter on Effective Communication)

Creativity: To think imaginatively and inventively.

If you are stuck in a traffic jam, do you accept the obstacle? Or do you draw on your creativity and think of possible alternatives? In other words, do you consider calling the control centre to let them know that you are on your way? Do you try to make your way to a different, less congested road? These creative ideas could help you overcome the obstacle and arrive at work on time. Creative minds figure out ways to overcome obstacles. You can look for creative ways, for instance, to organize your desk space to increase your efficiency.

In life, we often meet challenges and roadblocks. If I meet an irate customer who has been inconvenienced by a full parking lot, do I just let him know that the parking lot is full? Or do I use my creativity and suggest another carport where he can park? If a washroom is out of order, do I simply put up a sign that reads "Out of order?" Or do I use my creativity and attach to the sign the directions to another washroom?

Customer Service: To provide assistance to a person buying a product or a service.

If you worked in an automobile manufacturing plant, you would not be able to interact directly with the customer. You would not get the immediate rewards we get when we engage with our customers directly and face-to-face.

Who are our customers? This is an important question, and one that is more complex than it might seem. Our external customers include the owners of sites. Sometimes these owners are corporations. In addition, the tenants are often billed back for the services we provide. So they, too, are our customers. And their guests, by extension, are our customers, too. These external customers rely on our knowledge of our environment and they expect us to be personable and polite.

Not only do we get to interact with external customers and lift their spirits by assisting them, we also get involved with internal customers. Our teammates and our supervisors are our internal customers. And we become their customers, too, when we ask them for help. During hand-shakes, for instance, we become each other's customers, because we're giving each other assistance.

OK, that's enough on the "customer" for now. Let's think about the word "service." You recall the important distinction between products and services? To refresh your memory: whereas our expectations of products do not translate from one product to another, our increasingly high expectations of customer service do translate from one situation to another.

When a cab driver greets me politely, for instance, and helps me with my luggage, and drives me safely to my destination, I feel thankful for the service he has provided me, his customer. Because he has taken the time to clean his cab and to be friendly, he has brightened my day. I show my satisfaction with a tip. But let's say that I then go into an hotel and the front desk clerk does not even make eye-contact with me. What's more, he takes about five minutes to even acknowledge that I'm there and when he does, he gives me a blank look. I have to tell him that I'm there to check in, because otherwise we wouldn't communicate. Because the cab driver proved to me that excellent customer service does exist, he heightens my awareness of the hotel clerk's appalling customer service. This example illustrates once again that our customer service expectations translate from one situation to another. And they should. There's no reason not to provide premium customer service all the time.

Dedication: **To commit oneself to your work and/or to others. To devote yourself to a cause or a purpose**.

To be devoted means to be fully engaged in the present. You reveal your dedication by immersing yourselves in your tasks. Dedication involves commitment to a purpose that will require effort and time.

By dedicating yourself on a daily basis, you will eventually reach levels that you cannot imagine now. By making a promise to yourself to be committed to your work in the present moment, you will reap many unforeseeable benefits.

As the old saying goes, we reap what we sow. In our line of work, we show up at the site alert and attentive, we carry out our patrols, we observe and report, we learn the orders and procedures, and we fully apply ourselves. We then harvest our rewards: we advance in our careers, we receive the recognition and respect of our peers and our superiors, and we gain the trust of our clients. Clearly, being dedicated to our job functions allows us to reap many rewards.

A story that exemplifies creativity, excellent customer service, and the rewards of taking ownership:

A parking attendant working at a lot in B.C. decided to plant his own flowers to beautify the premises. He watered his garden and maintained it. In addition, he learned the names of his regular customers and he recognized their vehicles. He took the time to nurture the garden, making the otherwise bland landscape more inviting; he also took the time to nurture a friendly rapport with his customers. He took ownership of his job functions, finding ways to give his all to his work. He became a symbol of community service and people would drive out to the lot just to meet him and see his garden. For his efforts, the Building Owners and Managers Association (BOMA) of Canada presented the attendant at one of their prestigious ceremonies with a Pinnacle award.

Efficiency: To function effectively with little waste of time and effort.

We live in a very busy world. You save yourself and others time by communicating thoroughly and by writing thorough notes. The best way to be efficient is to think before you speak, write, and act. If you prepare and drill, you will perform efficiently and effectively when it's time to act. By reflecting and thinking about your actions you can analyze how you can change your actions so that you can perform them even more efficiently. You must reflect on how you do your patrols and tasks and whether there is room for you to make improvements. If so, incorporate these changes in your routines or at least communicate the need for change to your supervisor.

Keeping Honest People Honest.

The presence of security officers helps the most honest individual to stay honest. Sometimes minor acts of deceit seem trivial and unimportant. But every act of deceit has a consequence. And the presence of security officers is a reminder and an enforcer of the consequence.

If, for example, someone temporarily parks in a "handicapped" spot while they run into a store to buy a few groceries, the consequences seem fairly minimal as long as nobody is looking. However, if a security officer is strolling through the lot, the person will spend a few extra minutes to find an acceptable spot to park. They know they risk getting a ticket or having their car towed. The presence of a security guard reminds them that breaking the rules has consequences.

Ethics: The rules that govern our behavior and keep our integrity intact.

Your ethics are the support system to your **integrity**. Your code of ethics is the shield that protects your integrity, honour, and sense of self-worth. Falsifying reports, for instance, is an ethical issue. You can keep your integrity intact by reporting only factual information.

Your code of ethics ensures that you remain committed to what you believe is right. For example, you know it's wrong to drink and drive. It can have devastating consequences. Your code of ethics directs you not to do it.

Never Compromise Ethics/Protocols for the Sake of Making Something Happen More Quickly.

Being efficient is crucial in your job. Short cuts, as opposed to the scenic route, are often necessary to get from point A to point B in the fastest way. But you shouldn't take the shorter route if it means skipping the necessary processes and procedures involved in those tasks. Shortcuts are not excuses to be lazy. Time demands and the volume of work may seem unmanageable. But by taking each item one slice at a time—one phone call, one report, one patrol—the work will get done, I assure you! Find the necessary efficiencies in your work, but do not compromise the integrity of the task for a quick-fix solution.

When, for instance, you are providing access control, it is your responsibility to follow the required steps. These include checking photo ID to verify identity and check the access control databases to verify that the person is indeed permitted in the building. They may need a pass or an escort, but an impatient person who is running late for a meeting may suggest that you skip these steps. At the moment he arrives, you might be swamped with other tasks and it might be easier for both of you to let him proceed right away. But this shortcut is unacceptable. The policy of identification verification and database checking is a necessary precaution. You can lessen the guest's irritation by being friendly and efficient.

High Motivation: **To work with great enthusiasm. To exhibit great energy.**

NASS creates incentives and opportunities to heighten its employees' motivation. It creates environments that encourage us all to come to work with a smile. No matter how many incentives we create, however, motivation has to come from inside. It's up to you to come to work feeling enthusiastic and full of energy.

We are all unique individuals, each with his or her own strengths and weaknesses. We all have bad days. Day-to-day events can wear us down, making us feel depressed and less enthusiastic.

Traffic jams, family problems, financial struggles, health worries, are some of the factors that can dampen our enthusiasm. We must confront the issues that arise in our lives, but we must also look to a better tomorrow. And I'll share with you a secret that I've learned in the course of my life: *we ourselves create that better tomorrow.* We create our reality. We have a chance to be heroic when our friends feel down, because we can motivate them. By sharing our enthusiasm with others, we create a better, happier reality for ourselves.

Innovation: The introduction of new ideas and methods.

An innovation usually involves an improvement to a process. An innovation also usually involves the coming together of many *creative* minds.

Let's consider the following example: During a fire alarm, people must evacuate to a containment area. Imagine that the evacuation area is outdoors. What will people do if the evacuation has to take place in the middle of winter? Our managers might connect with the managers of a neighboring building to agree to use each other's lobbies as containment areas. Obviously, it's better to have this agreement before you have to organize an evacuation. This is an example of an innovative solution based on cooperation and teamwork between neighbors.

In our company, we're known for our innovations. They are demonstrated in our staffing procedures, our HR system, our stand-by pool for staff, our uniform components and in our VPN (Virtual Private Network). We are, and will continue to be, an innovative company because we provide a working environment where innovative people can bring their ideas forward.

Integrity: The quality of being honest, uncompromising and moral.

As individuals, I believe that our integrity is the most precious thing we have. Simply put: if you compromise your integrity, your self-worth decreases. Your values are constantly tested throughout your life. You have to confront temptations.

Why not steal the jewelry that you are meant to be securing? Because you know it's wrong and you can police yourself. During a late night patrol, why not help yourself to something you like? Because your own internal police will know you did it.

It's not only the fear of being caught that stops us. We know that doing wrong is not the way we want to make our mark in life. We want to live with a clear conscience; we want to keep our integrity intact.

Sometimes your integrity is tested in more subtle ways. Imagine that you are working the overnight shift: Do you really want to do all your patrols? Would anyone notice if you skipped one? Let's say that there were ways to circumvent the checks and balances. If you do not go on patrol and you therefore miss something smoldering, will you be able to live with yourself afterwards? If you don't do the patrol, and there are consequences, you are accountable for them.

These tough questions can challenge your integrity. Do you look the other way, or do you stand your ground? Do you report the wrongdoing of your co-worker? By not reporting a wrongful act, do you know that you are conspiring with your co-worker in the wrongdoing? You are paid *not* to look the other way.

Our jobs involve keeping honest people honest. If you falsify reports, you commit fraud. You lose your integrity. Sometimes we make mistakes, but one way of reclaiming our integrity in these situations is to own up and be accountable for them. We're all human and sometimes there are valid reasons why things don't get done. By owning up to our mistakes we reclaim our integrity and demonstrate that we are accountable, trustworthy employees.

Not reporting a mistake is another mistake.

Mishaps

Accidents happen. An unexpected mishap is acceptable, and in most cases it is reversible. It is critical, however, that you tell your supervisor about the mishap immediately, either verbally or in a written report.

Failure to report the mishap, or an attempt to hide the mistake or to lie about the situation, is unacceptable. An employer will see the second error in judgment (hiding the mishap) as an intentional act of deceit. As security officers, we are in positions of trust. **An act of deceit such as hiding a mistake will provoke an employer to question the security officer's credibility.** Deceit is no way to further a career; it doesn't work. Being honest from the start—admitting to the mishap—shows the employer that he/she can trust you. We must never make a second mistake by hiding the first one.

Long hours working in pairs often leads co-workers to become friends. Co-workers who have become friends must not hide each other's mistakes. While on the job, the company's ethics—the policies, processes, and procedures--are your moral fibre. They are the rules we all live by. If a co-worker or a friend bends the rules, it's your duty to inform him/her that he or she was wrong. If it's a minor infraction and a one-time occurrence, a reminder might be all it takes to ensure that the co-worker won't bend the rules again. Acting as a mentor is an important part of being a good friend. In addition, it's part of your job. Good advice could save your friend's job!

If your co-worker repeatedly breaks rules, it is your responsibility to report his/her actions. While you might feel that you are betraying a good friend, a good friend would not put you in a position in which you have to choose between them and your job.

When you report your co-worker, your manager will take note of your admirable understanding of right and wrong, and your courage in choosing integrity over dishonesty.

Mentoring: Guiding and advising another person.

Every employee in the company adopts the role of mentor at some point or another. In other words, each of us uses his strengths to guide our teammates. Since each of us feels more comfortable with some processes that are less familiar to some of our teammates, we can coach them in these processes. For example, you can mentor a new employee by showing him how to use the stretcher to move disabled people to a fire exit. Although we have stored much of our accumulated corporate knowledge on TeamNet, we still rely on the buddy system because often new employees are overwhelmed by the amount of information they must absorb. We have created a buddy system that partners a veteran and a rookie. The veteran offers tips, and provides support and comfort to the rookie.

At NASS, we're very interested in having our supervisors show teammates how to do things correctly. We hire employees knowing that they want to learn the correct processes and procedures. Since each staff member consistently looks at how he/she can add value to their services, their willingness to learn makes coaching a central, pleasurable, community-enhancing aspect of our company.

Leading by Example

As security officers, we are also role models. If, for instance, you smoke, you do so only in the designated area and encourage guests to smoke in the designated area. If, however, you smoke in the lobby of the building before heading outside, guests will feel that they, too, can break the rules. **It's impossible to enforce a rule that you feel *you* are above.**

Even if a certain procedure isn't written in stone, it's important for the security officer to set a good example. Cigarette butts, for instance, should be disposed of in the proper manner.

At shopping centres, staff are encouraged to park furthest away from the building in order to leave the closer spaces for customers. Security officers do the same. We can only enforce the rules that *we* ourselves obey. **We must obey the rules that we enforce.**

Multi-Tasking: To work on many assignments, charges, and duties side by side, in parallel.

Imagine the following situation: you are at your desk, and a walk-up customer approaches you hoping that you will help them to find their way (remember, giving directions is one of the key aspects of our job-function). At that exact moment the customer approaches your desk, the telephone rings.

What do you do? You have two competing demands for your time. Here is the answer that you may have thought of. You pick up the phone--after **gesturing** to the walk-up customer to wait for one second. You have greeted the person at your desk: "Good morning/afternoon/evening. One moment please." Then you answer the phone and you say **"Good afternoon. This is security. If this is not an urgent matter, could you please hold for a brief moment? I'm dealing with a walk-up customer."**

What's happened? You have attended to both the walk-up customer and the customer on the phone. Now the walk-up customer knows that if you continue to talk on the phone, you are dealing with an emergency and he/she will likely give you time to deal with the urgent matter. You have acknowledged that the walk-up customer is important. You have shown them that you want to help them as soon as you can. In addition, the person on the phone knows that you're busy and that you are not engaged in a routine matter. So, if their situation is not urgent, they will be more likely to wait patiently while you attend to the walk-up customer. Both customers should understand the situation and be patient.

Multi-tasking means being able to perform more than one task **WELL**. How do you do everything well without making any person or task seem secondary? We deal with people and tasks one at a time, according to priority. Just as hospitals deal with their patients in order of urgency, you should tend to life-threatening emergencies before routine tasks. If there is no emergency, deal with the tasks in sequential order, on a first-come, first-served basis. **Ongoing Training: To continue to learn, grow, direct, aim and guide.**

The only constant in life is change. To retain our competitive edge, personally and as a company, we have to practice the skills we know, as well as constantly learn new ones. If we stand still and the rest of the world is moving, the net effect is the same as going backwards.

Consider the following example: Ten years ago we taught our staff Level A CPR for adults. In the late 1990s, we incorporated a program on how to do CPR on teenagers. Then we began training our staff on how to perform CPR on children. We continually raised the bar. Today, we use Automated External Defibrillators (AEDs). These are quickly becoming standard equipment. With AEDs, we now have an additional option for resuscitating cardiac arrest victims.

Ongoing training is exciting and rewarding, but it demands **discipline** and **dedication** on your part. It will require some effort to learn new skills, but the personal and professional return on investment will be well worth it.

Quality-Mindedness: To think and behave in terms of excellence.

What is quality? In the old days we used to think that hiring excellent staff was all that we needed to do to achieve quality. Yes, we still want to hire the best staff we can. But we also want them to have great uniforms, to learn clear work processes, to provide good leadership, to reinforce a good support system, and to nurture good partnerships with our clients.

Over the years, as the company developed and grew, we started to reflect on our cumulative years of corporate knowledge. We began to ask how we could properly evaluate processes. For example, we realized that a better patrol technique for large office towers would involve zig-zagging down the floors, doing four floors at a time and then checking the lobby. Over time, we re-evaluated the traditional patrol method, and introduced a better technique and a better way of approaching the work. Over time we develop better policies, processes, and procedures, systems and techniques.

In addition to reevaluating processes and improving them, quality also involves consistency. Let's consider the following: nine out of the 10 days that you work you follow the system. During one of these days, you're distracted. The overall quality of your work drops. You undermine the excellent quality of the work you did during those nine days because you're not focused on that one, distracted day. By working systematically, however, you can retain the high quality of our work. In other words, by applying your processes and your procedures, and by executing the techniques that you have drilled so many times, even on that one bad day, you get consistent results that retain your high quality of work.

> *"I don't see Quality as one person, one department or one vendor. Quality is a mindset. To move the yardstick, it requires support and partnership at all levels. The little things that people see, the processes with which they work, the ownership they have are all part of the Quality program.*
>
> *People want quality, yet they don't know what quality is. They want to buy it like a cup of coffee at Tim Hortons. They want it yesterday. But quality is like a person's garden. It requires time, water, sun, shade, fertilizer, and true tender loving care by its owner.*
>
> *We prove quality in a tried, tested, true way. The GM model also speaks true for quality. Using a model to work with what you have today and to work with the team to make it better one step at a time. If I look at the NASS office: when a staff member walks into our lobby, is it clean and neat? Is the paint fresh? When staff members walk by, do they put the chairs back, do they pick up somebody's left behind garbage? When you go into our washroom, if it's out of paper towels, do you refresh the container? When you take your vehicle for service, how do you explain what's wrong? Do you take the time to get the facts, the root cause, or do you just complain? If you complain with no facts and no root cause, you don't understand Quality.*
>
> *Quality is about the details, the little details.*
>
> *Quality is taking the time to slow down to the speed of life and it's taking the time to care."*
>
> *Kevin Cooney, Vice President, NASS*

Reliability: Being consistently dependable. Showing others they can always depend on us to follow up on our word.

Being reliable involves showing up for work on time and following through on your responsibilities. Reliability also involves taking ownership of your tasks. At NASS, we look for dependable staff. Experience has shown that nothing is as good an indication of future performance as past performance. By showing up to work on time again and again, over the period of a year, for instance, you show your supervisors that you are reliable. They should know they can rely on you to arrive to work at least 15 minutes early.

And you also expect the company to be reliable. You bank on receiving a cheque from NASS every two weeks. Because we meet your expectations time and time again, you learn that you can trust us.

Similarly, you give your supervisors peace of mind by showing them, time and time again, that you consistently follow processes. In other words, they know they can rely on you not to let every tenth person through access control without being scrutinized.

When you consistently follow processes, your dependability also gives the tenants of the building a sense of comfort. They know they can rely on you to maintain the building's security. The tenants feel safe because they know they can rely on you to look out for fire and safety hazards. Your dependability gives them the benefit of peace of mind.

Resourcefulness: Having a reservoir of tools. Building up skill sets. Developing these skill sets.

As you work, you build a repertoire of skills that you can draw on when challenges arise. Faced with a problem, you reach into your back pockets to pull out tricks, tools, and resources. Your resources include your fellow team members and your supervisors. But they're not your only resources. When you need guidance you can also look to SmartNet. It is your twenty-four hour resource. If you need information on the eight-step de-escalation process, for example, you can turn to the VPN. But you can't think of doing this at the moment of a confrontation; because that's the wrong time to wonder how to deal with the situation. By filling your resource toolbox continuously, and by re-sharpening your tools and mentally (as well as physically) drilling your skills, your resources are immediately available to you when you need them. They become a part of your being. Remember that building the necessary reserve of tools will take persistence and time.

Teamwork: Cooperation and interaction of a team. A supportive group of people working together on a project. Encouraging each other during a challenge.

Teamwork is a big subject. Working with others expands our lives. Whether in our work or in our social relationships, teamwork involves remembering the following: **Not any one of us knows as much as all of us do.** In our line of work, we often work in isolation. But we're never alone: we're all connected through the VPN and through hand-offs, for example. Although your shift may end, you hand-off responsibility to your team member, and it's through a collective effort that we preserve the integrity of the site and secure it.

Also, remember the following: **We're only as strong as our weakest link.** We are part of a large team and we are accountable to one another. Just as your team-members count on you, so you count on them. Communicate your expectations. During a bike ride with friends recently, my teammates' encouraging words enabled me to cycle a little longer and a little harder. Another time, it might be my turn to take the lead and push my friends to go further. At NASS, each staff member brings unique strengths that others can benefit from.

To be heroic means working together and taking proactive and preventative measures. We focus on the collective approach. I grew up in the Batman era: When the mayor of Gotham city turned on the Batlight, I (identifying myself with Batman), would fantasize that I was rushing to save Gotham City. Whether your hero is Batman, James Bond, or Lara Croft, we all have dreams of being heroic. But being heroic does not mean doing it alone. **It means anticipating problems and working actively, not reactively.** One way of being heroic is to train others on your team to be as good as you are. Remember that we're only as strong as our weakest link. **We become heroic by helping our teammates to be heroic in creating "non-events."** We focus on fire-prevention rather than on fire-fighting. Some decades ago, we only had fire brigades that responded to fires. Today, we emphasize fire-codes and fire-prevention inspectors and try to avoid the need for fire brigades.

True heroism involves coaching, teamwork, and prevention. Remember, even Batman relied on Robin, James Bond looked to M and Q, Lara Croft has her IT team. Heroism also involves avoiding havoc: someone always had to pick up the broken pieces of Gotham City. **We can idealize these fictional characters, but in the real world we reach heroic stature by incorporating** our cooperative, preventative approach into a corporate environment.

> **T**ogether
> **E**veryone
> **A**chieves
> **M**ore

Chapter Ten
Leadership Strategies

"Example is not the main thing in influencing others. It's the only thing."

Albert Schweitzer, Nobel Peace Prize Winner, 1952

"When you learn, teach. When you get, give."

Maya Angelou, writer and activist

At NASS, we train our leaders to have a vision of the future. We favour active, creative visionaries over reactive, in-the-box managers. Our leadership team guides, mentors, encourages, and motivates our staff. We don't need managers: Our policies, processes and procedures manage *us*. If we have a management problem, we look at how we can better our process.

The great majority of our leaders have grown within the company and moved up the ranks. Most of them joined NASS as security officers. Growing in the company has reinforced their understanding of NASS' corporate culture. Since we all continue to grow and expand throughout our lives, NASS offers "Train the Trainers" and "Lessons Learned" workshops throughout the year. The leadership team must attend these workshops but they are open to all. In the past, we've seen that the employees who attend these workshops are the ones who are most likely to be promoted in the company. You can register for these workshops online, through NASS' VPN.

Leadership Strategies

1. Personnel: Our leadership team screens, selects, and recruits the best candidates, and these individuals tend to show a real drive to develop. By overloading themselves—by functioning according to the logic of positive pressure—they grow as individuals and as security officers. NASS leaders have a genuine interest in helping current staff prepare for promotion and higher levels of responsibility. These candidates continue to develop throughout their employment with NASS.

2. Training: At NASS, we constantly improve our training curriculum and evaluation procedures to ensure that we have better than industry-standard staff. Most companies will give a pass to new security officers who achieve a minimum of 75 percent on their training exams. Until a few years ago, NASS would pass only officers who achieved at least 80 percent on these exams. It didn't take us long to realize that we could no longer accept 80 percent as a minimum pass mark. Doing so meant sending security officers into the field who lacked 20 percent of the required knowledge. Today we continue to train new employees (on the 20 percent that they initially missed) until they complete their exam perfectly—with a grade of 100 percent! That way, we ensure that they arrive on-site with a full understanding of the fundamentals.

3. Communication: To my knowledge, we are the *only* physical security provider in North America that enables our clients, their clients, all our security personnel, and our management team to communicate "virtually" and in real time. Our HR and operational virtual processes and tools distinguish us from our competitors. Because we have more premium staff, and excellent communication to direct our staff, we remain at the forefront of the industry.

4. Coaching: NASS nurtures leaders, not managers. We empower the leadership staff, who in turn learn to guide and mentor our employees. We encourage them to show vision and creativity. NASS' investment in training its leaders helps them progress faster and reinforces their confidence.

Because we have a high percentage of highly trained security officers, visionary leaders, and innovative, user-friendly communication processes, we remain very competitive in the security industry. Applying these strategies ensures our competitiveness in the marketplace.

System Solutions

Like all organizations, NASS must deal with the human condition. Illness, family obligations, vacation requests, staff turnovers and last-minute client requests teach us to expect and adapt to the unexpected. While we can predict that security officers will occasionally be unable to come to work, we cannot predict "where" or "when" or "why." We must be prepared to deal at any time with an un-forecasted employee absence.

NASS has found a proactive way to get to the root of the problem. We've developed a "system solution." Here's an illustration of how it works: If a client needs 400 hours a week of regular security officer services, NASS will schedule the client's directed staffing requirement. But we don't stop there. We realize that scheduling only the directed personnel does not take the human condition into account. If we merely meet the requirements, we might have to scramble to find extra staff at the last minute.

To combat the problem, NASS makes it a regular practice to up-staff each site to predetermined levels—in most cases we up-staff an additional 15 percent. To continue with this example, we would organize a back-up system of 60 security hours, including a stand-by pool of fully trained personnel ready at a moment's notice, and an on-call pool. By always providing surplus staff for all sites, we reduce stress levels and increase productivity.

NASS has targeted and eliminated the effects of absenteeism at the root cause level. By dealing with it as a process solution, we are able to meet our clients' standards and maintain a high level of employee satisfaction.

Follow-Ups

If I assign a task, I expect a supervisor to complete it by the end of his or her shift. If it can't be completed by that time, the supervisor must inform me as soon as possible. I need to know why the task wasn't completed, how to fix the problem causing the delay, and when the task will be complete. The leader and I have the shared responsibility of communicating. If we need to revise the deadline, we do. If the leader does not communicate a need for a new deadline, I assume the task can and will be completed by the end of the day.

During a supervisor's first few weeks on the job, it used to be quite common for him or her to get a call from me before bedtime.

"I'm in bed," I would say, no doubt surprising the supervisor, who hadn't expected to hear from me at that hour. "But I can't sleep yet because you didn't get back to me about finishing X,Y or Z."

In most cases, the supervisor had completed the task but had forgotten to close the loop by letting me know. If they hadn't completed the task, I would expect them to tell me why.

Satisfied, I would then reply: "Thank you. Goodnight."

By following up like this, I wasn't really being a difficult boss. I was trying to encourage a habit of mind that all employees should follow. Plus, I really can't sleep without knowing how the work is going. I need employee communication to get a good night's rest. As a result of my calls, my supervisors—many of whom have been with NASS now for over a decade—have instilled this practice in their support teams. (I am so proud of them.) NASS employees quickly learn that deadlines are important, work is important, and closure must be achieved by the end of the day, unless they are told otherwise.

Giving Feedback

My dad used to say: "They will respect what you inspect." I tell my staff that if the work is important, we should be supervising, measuring, and reviewing it. And we must be concise and constructive when we give employees feedback on their reports.

Corridor Meetings

Corridor meetings are forums where you can discuss issues in an informal way. Passing a co-worker in a corridor can remind you of an important issue that you had temporarily put on the backburner. It's an ideal opportunity to mention a worrisome problem without the pressure to come up with an immediate solution. If you take a positive approach, you'll probably get a positive response. You may not always get the outcome you want, but your opinion is always valued. Corridor meetings are also great opportunities to give a co-worker a pat on the back for a job well done.

Brainstorming Not "Blamestorming"

You've heard the expression: "Misery loves company." Some people say that, as social beings, we enhance a feeling of connectedness with others by sharing our frustrations with them. But why do people feel that they can only connect with one another by venting about a common problem? Why can't employees bond by sharing their *positive* thoughts? I've seen how a negative conversation among peers can suck in even their positive colleagues. Negativity is a virus. And like a virus, negativity weakens us.

More than once I have come across a gathering of security officers having a smoke or a coffee and grumbling about something. Rather than discuss the excellent plays in last night's hockey game, they complain about the expensive parking and their poor seats. Negativity breeds more negativity.

When I hear staff complaining about some aspects of their jobs, I approach the group and ask them to propose some meaningful solutions. They are usually silenced by my request. Only when I persist will a member of the group finally bring the issue to light. Because I'm their boss, and they don't want to criticize a policy I approved, they tend to talk about it more optimistically when I'm around. Why couldn't they address it in the same positive way with their co-workers? Instead of complaining, the group could have used the cigarette break as an opportunity to brainstorm solutions. A positive attitude is also contagious, and can be wonderful.

Thinking positively improves your physical and psychological health. It also increases your energy. Thinking creatively about ways to solve problems is a skill that needs to be developed. Being able to move beyond certain frustrations, rather than fixate on them, gives you more time to focus on getting the necessary protocols done. If you do come up with a good idea or a better way, share your idea!

When To *Stop* Meeting In The Corridor

While the informality of a corridor meeting is fine for some situations, there must be a structured system for employees to air their complaints. Of course, the system must also include a platform for positive comments! If you have something you want management to know, bring it to your supervisor. If you're not satisfied with the supervisor's response, go to the next level of management.

NASS has built a suggestion box into its VPN, which can be accessed through TeamNet. The quick link is available on every page of SmartNet, which allows you to efficiently communicate your thoughts.

Small problems, if not attended to, can easily grow into larger ones and can lead to general dissatisfaction, low morale, and poor performance. (If you don't think small problems can have big consequences, try going to sleep with a mosquito in your room.) You *can* make procedural or operational suggestions. You can also offer your ideas on how to improve our processes, including the VPN. If you approach your supervisor in the right way, your issue will get the attention it deserves.

To-Do Lists

I believe in writing things down. I suggest that all NASS supervisors take up the same practice and make "to-do" lists. This kind of list is a constant reminder of important and time-sensitive tasks. With the "Internet-speed of society," we can forget our thoughts as quickly as they come to us. By making a list, and referring to it throughout the day, supervisors can avoid forgetting an important task. When the list is complete, the supervisor can choose to do more, that is, to go above and beyond what is expected of him or her.

Murphy's Law says that everything that can go wrong, *will* go wrong. You can't afford to let things slip through the cracks—your neglect could have serious consequences. A to-do list ensures that the cracks are covered so that nothing escapes your attention. NASS supervisors check off the tasks on their list as they accomplish them. At the end of their shift, they start a new list containing any uncompleted tasks. Some people prioritize their lists, placing the most important and time-sensitive tasks at the top.

The process sounds easy because it really is, but many people underestimate its importance. Pertinent information must be recorded for reference and reminder. And it must be done consistently. The supervisor who makes it a ritual to follow a "to-do" list will seldom be disappointed.

It's possible to send a message via SmartNet that immediately triggers a *"follow-up"* request on the recipient's home page. This feature encourages a two-way flow of communication between staff and helps you complete all the tasks on your list efficiently.

Furthermore, NASS has developed a feature on SmartNet that automatically creates *"action items"* or to do lists for its supervisors and managers, ensuring *closure* to any outstanding items.

Clarity of Working Instructions

Imagine that you are a security officer on a temporary assignment who has been instructed to "bar entry" to an office. What does this instruction mean, exactly? Six employees are physically present in the office. If one of them leaves, can he re-enter? Should you kick out all six workers? Can the workers bring in escorted guests? Is upper management permitted in the area?

Obviously, this work instruction is too vague. Poorly worded instructions, by the way, are a major problem in our industry. Since the instructions are open to interpretation, each security officer will filter the message through his or her personality screen and interpret it in his or her own way. If the officer doesn't ask for clarification, there could be serious consequences. We must give our security officers clear and detailed working instructions.

Multi-Tasking (Again)

In today's world, the ability to focus has become more important than ever. People must now have the ability to focus on many tasks at the same time. And each task requires the same level of attentiveness and care. To complete tasks at the same time we must work on them in parallel and in conjunction.

We must give the same kind of care to each task that the ancient artists and masons gave to each tiny pebble in the beautiful mosaics I saw in Rome. Attentiveness, friendliness, and a focused, result-oriented effort will lead to outstanding results.

Chapter Eleven
Further Inspiration

"If a man is called to be a streetsweeper, he should sweep streets as Michelangelo painted, or Beethoven composed music, or Shakespeare wrote poetry. He should sweep streets so well that all the hosts of heaven and earth will pause to say, here lived a great streetsweeper who did his job well."

Martin Luther King Jr.

Life's Little Instructions

Compliment at least three people every day.
Treat everyone you meet like you want to be treated.
Look people in the eye.
Be kinder than necessary.
Say thank you often.
Be the first to say "hello."
Compliment even small improvements.
Practice random acts of kindness.

Learn three clean jokes.
Learn CPR.
Carry jumper cables in your trunk.
Wear polished shoes.
Have a firm handshake.

Remember other people's birthdays.
Make new friends but cherish old ones.
Rekindle old friendships.
Focus on making things better, not bigger.
Be there when people need you.

Strive for excellence, not perfection.
Become the most positive and enthusiastic person you know.
Be forgiving of yourself and others.
Commit yourself to constant improvement.
Stop blaming others…

...Take responsibility for every area in your life.
Keep your promises.

Return borrowed vehicles with the gas tank full.
Leave everything a little better than you found it.
Return all things you borrow.
Think big thoughts but relish small pleasures.
Take good care of those you love.
Don't postpone joy.
Become someone's hero.
Take time to smell the roses.
Count your blessings.

Did You Know?

During medieval times, a dinner invitation, even from a best friend, could be dangerous. To prove that the wine was safe, the host would clink his pewter mug with his guest, allowing some of the liquid from each cup to splash between the mugs. The drinkers would take their first sips while staring into each other's eyes, to ensure that they drank at the same moment. Today, the clinking of glasses goes with a toast. The tradition of toasting, then, stems from a security measure! Although the custom of testing for poison while drinking wine at a dinner party is no longer necessary, the need for private security measures remains.

Did You Know?

The Middle Ages were a dangerous period, and those with valuables to protect barricaded themselves in castles. Such fortresses were equipped with physical obstacles, like moats and drawbridges. In addition, knights often surveyed the interior from carefully situated look-out points. Although we no longer build castles, moats, and drawbridges, we see modern equivalents of these everywhere.

We can regard a large corporation headquarters as a modern castle. We use the most advanced perimeter protection to keep enemies from gaining access to valuable property, such as high-tech equipment and information. Today's defences include electromagnetic access cards, security cameras watching from above and alarm systems. Security officers are the modern knights.

Did You Know?

Before the railroads went west, stagecoaches were the primary means of transportation. The stagecoach had a driver who sat at the front of the coach and another person, a guard, who sat "shotgun." The person riding shotgun protected both the passengers and any goods that were being transported. This security measure evolved, and with the expansion of the railway, armed personnel were hired to guard the cash car.

In modern times, the armoured car was designed to protect valuable goods. Personal security officers still protect people who are at risk of being attacked. As we can see, security is not a dying art. The primary purpose of security officers continues to be the protection of people and valuables. There will always be a need for security services. As security officers we are part of a long-standing tradition and we can take pride in our profession.

In today's society, where police services are stretched to the limit, many times it is the men and women who work as security officers who are called upon to make safe and secure our property, workplace, shopping malls, hospitals, and even sometimes our children. To say that it is a growing industry would be an understatement. One only has to look at the condominiums being built, with most of them offering security 24-7.

Employees of North American Security Services (NASS), who are also members of UCFW Local 206, are a conscientious, dedicated group of people, who are continually on course to better serve the client and the public. We are proud to represent these employees, working in an industry that historically has not given them the recognition they deserve.

However, we are also of the opinion that changes are forthcoming. As public awareness of security grows, so will the demand for trained qualified personnel. Given time, we have no doubt that the people who work in the security industry will finally receive the appreciation they deserve, and that in the not so distant future, being a security officer will not just be viewed as a job. It will be considered a career.

Frank G. Kelly, Vice President, UFCW